THE NEW ALDINE LIBRARY

VI. THE LITTLE BROWN COMPANY

THE LITTLE BROWN COMPANY: AN ANTHOLOGY OF FRANCISCAN POETRY & PROSE GATHERED BY LOUIS VINCENT

LONDON: MARTIN HOPKINSON AND COMPANY LTD. 14 HENRIETTA STREET, COVENT GARDEN, W.C. 1925

PRINTED IN GREAT BRITAIN BY ROBERT MACLEHOSE AND CO. LTD.
THE UNIVERSITY PRESS, GLASGOW

FOREWORD

A FRANCISCAN Anthology might, and perhaps should, be a weighty and scholarly tome filled with gleanings from the rich field of the world's Franciscan literature. Limitations of time and talent apart, I have preferred the smaller and more popular way as that best suited my purpose. I have been less concerned with literary and poetic grace than finding the true expression of the Franciscan spirit. Nevertheless I hope the reader will agree that the quality is up to the level of the great theme, or harmony of themes, that makes Franciscanism the most alluring of all the Catholic Church's fragrant avenues of holiness.

L. V.

CONTENTS

1. The Singing Saint - - - *J. B. Morton*
2. The Franciscan Purpose - - *Matthew Arnold*
3. Of Holy Poverty - - - *Jacopone da Todi*
   (*Translation by Mrs. Theodore Beck*)
4. How two old men showed the
   Blessed Francis where he
   might find the Lady Poverty - " *The Lady Poverty* "
   (*Translation, Mr. Montgomery Carmichael*)
5. Assisi - - - - - *Father H. E. G. Rope, M.A.*
6. The Acolade - - - - *G. K. Chesterton*
7. Our Lady of the Angels - - *Trans. by Alan G. M'Dougall*
8. The City of St. Francis - - *E. Hutton*
9. The Cloister - - - - *Charles L. O'Donnell, C.S.C.*
10. Of the Sojourn of My Lady
    Poverty with the Brothers - " *The Lady Poverty* "
    (*Translation, Mr. Montgomery Carmichael*)
11. St. Francis to the Birds - - *Katharine Tynan Hinkson*
12. How St. Francis taught Brother
    Leo how to answer him - *The Fioretta*
13. The Mendicant - - - *Enid Dinnis*
14. The Joyous Penitents - - *Paul Sabatier (Translation)*
15. The Lady Poverty - - - *Alice Meynell*
16. The Sacramental Sign - *Father Cuthbert, O.S.F.C.*
17. Our Lord Christ of Order - *St. Francis (adapted, D. G. Rossetti)*
18. The Golden Sayings of Brother
    Giles - - - - - *Father Paschal Robinson, O.F.M.*
19. St. Francis and Perfect Joy - *Aubrey De Vere*
20. Renunciation - - - - *John Ruskin*

vii

CONTENTS

21. Cor Dulce - - - - *Katharine Tynan Hinkson*
22. The Vision Splendid - - *Rev. H. F. B. Mackay*
23. Brother Ass and St. Francis - *J. B. Tabb*
24. St. Francis' Salutation of the Virtues - - - - *Father Paschal Robinson, O.F.M.*
25. The Ascent - - - - *Father H. E. G. Rope*
26. How Brother Fire dealt gently with God's Servant - - *Legenda St. Bonaventure* (*Translation, Miss Lockhart*)
27. A Portrait - - - - *Nancy Dustan*
28. The Portrait of **St.** Francis - *Louis Gillet*
29. Portrait of St. Francis - - *Thomas Celano*
30. Sorrow - - - - - *Helen Parry Eden*
31. The Right to be Poor - - *Father Cuthbert, O.S.F.C.*
32. The Sermon of St. Francis - *H. D. Longfellow*
33. How the Blood flowed afresh from the Effigy of St. Francis *Ensamples and Miracles.* (*Version of M. Mansfield, " The Garden Inclosed "*)
34. Dun Scotus's Oxford - - *G. M. Hopkins*
35. Franciscan Gossip - - - *Thomas of Eccleston* (*Translation, Father Cuthbert, O.S.F.C.*)
36. A Franciscan Dream - - *Enid Dinnis*
37. In Praise of Poverty - - *Madeleine Nightingale*
38. The Singing Saint - - - *Sister Mary Benaventure, O.P.*
39. Knights of the Round Table - *Father Cuthbert, O.S.F.C.*
40. The Little Black Hen - - *Armel O'Connor*
41. St. Anthony of Padua - - *Father Dominic Devas, O.F.M.*
42. Appreciation à la Mode - - *Armel O'Connor*
43. The Begging Friar - - - *John Ruskin*
44. Ode on the Visit of St. Francis to the Holy Land - - *Father Adrian, O.F.M.*
45. Commemoration - - - *Rev. H. F. B. Mackay*
46. The Irish Franciscan - - *Rosa Mulholland (Lady Gilbert)*

viii

CONTENTS

47. Christmas at Greccio - - *Johannes Jörgensen*
      (*Translation, Mr. T. O'Connor Sloane*)
48. The Stigmata of St. Francis - *Father Adrian, O.F.M.*
49. Feast of the Stigmata - - *Montgomery Carmichael*
50. Democracies - - - - *W. E. Awde*
51. The Social Teaching of St.
      Francis - - - - *Father Cuthbert, O.S.F.C.*
52. At Assisi - - - - *Madeleine Nightingale*
53. Franciscan Art - - - *John Ruskin*
54. Paradiso - - - - *Dante*
55. The Blessing of Brother Leo - *Father Paschal Robinson,
            O.F.M.*
56. A Franciscan Prayer - - *Enid Dinnis*
57. The Sacristan's Cell - - *John Ruskin*
58. Canticle of the Sun - - *St. Francis*
      (*Father Paschal Robinson's Version*)
59. Deus Meus et Omnia - - *R. E.*
60. The Example of Brother Leo - *The Fioretta*
61. Mount Alvernia - - - *Father H. E. G. Rope*
62. St. Francis's Farewell to Mount
      La Verna - - - - *Montgomery Carmichael*
63. With Love on Mount Alvernia *Armel O'Connor*
64. Aurea Dicta - - - - *Coventry Patmore*
65. Founding of the Franciscan
      Monastery, Donegal - - *Leo*
66. The Lady St. Clare - - *Mrs. C. Balfour*
67. Of St. Francis and the Ass - *Katharine Tynan Hinkson*
68. The Death of St. Francis - *G. K. Chesterton*
69. After Strain - - - - *Francis Thompson*
70. St. Francis and the World - *Louis Vincent*
71. Of Impatience - - - *Jacopone da Todi*
72. Farewell to Assisi - - *Johannes Jörgenson*
73. A Prayer to the Humble on
      Earth - - - - - *Father Adrian, O.F.M.*
74. Prayers said on the Feast of
      St. Francis - - - - *The Missal*

ix

INTRODUCTION

MR. LOUIS VINCENT'S delightful anthology comes at an opportune moment when throughout Christendom the followers and admirers of the Seraphic Francis are preparing to commemorate the seventh centenary of the Saint's death. To Francis death was " our sister, bodily Death " ; no dark fate but a tender figure graciously opening the portals of the life eternal to the wearied yet joyous earth-wanderer. And therein we have an indication of the true Franciscan spirit. No man perhaps suffered more than did Saint Francis—whether by way of mental or bodily suffering ; yet was he a joyous sufferer, for was he not suffering in intimate companionship with Christ, the Lord and Redeemer of the earth ? Like Christ his Divine Master, Francis loved the earth and all that made up its glory, for was it not God's work and a witness to the Divine Power and majesty and to the Infinite Love which created it ? And because he loved it he would suffer with it, taking upon himself its iniquity as did Christ the Redeemer. Therefore was his suffering a joyous suffering—the suffering of one who loves and suffers for love and whose faith cannot be quenched. And Francis' faith both in God and in man was immense. Disillusions—and he suffered bitter disillusions—might

torture his faith in man, but could never destroy it. Sin
and misery might mar the beauty of God's earth, but
Francis never ceased to see its beauty. To the end he
was the joyous lover, idealising and worshipping, though
he suffered so much in his love.

As was Francis so was " the little brown company "
of which he was the leader and inspiration—not all, it
is true, in the same degree or purity of tone : and because
they were what they were—though cynics and the dis-
believing thought them fools—they helped a weary world
to regain both joy and faith.

FATHER CUTHBERT, O.S.F.C.

WOULD I might wake St. Francis in you all,
   Brother of birds and trees, God's Troubadour,
Blinded with weeping for the sad and poor :
Our wealth undone, all strict Franciscan men,
Come, let us chant the canticle again
Of mother earth and the enduring sun.
God make each soul the lowly leper's slave :
God make us saints, and brave.

VACHEL LINDSAY.

From " Collected Poems," Copyright 1923
by the Macmillan Co.

THE LITTLE BROWN COMPANY

I

The Singing Saint

ST. Francis walked in Umbria
    Seven hundred years ago ;
His soul was gladdened at the sight
Of those strong hills, where all the night
The fireflies dance, and silver light
    Gleams where the olives grow.

With lowly men in Umbria
    He sang the sweet refrains
Of Southern songs that lift the heart,
He preached the Faith in Church and mart,
Until the skies were torn apart,
    And Christ walked in the plains.

The little man of Umbria
    He praised with all his might
The Lord who made the little things,
Who fashioned birds with beating wings,
And slaked the earth with water-springs,
    And dowered with stars the night.

The faith he found in Umbria
    He taught it to the throng ;
For emblem of the Faith he took
Not lowered eyes and solemn look,
Nor frozen heart, nor printed book,
    But laughter and loud song.

J. B. MORTON

A   I

2

The Franciscan Purpose

IN the beginning of the thirteenth century, when the clouds and storms had come, when the gay sensuous pagan life was gone, when men were not living by the senses and understanding, when they were looking for the speedy coming of Antichrist, there appeared in Italy, to the north of Rome, in the beautiful Umbrian Country, at the foot of the Apennines, a figure of the most magical power and charm, St. Francis. This century is, I think, the most interesting in the history of Christianity after its primitive age . . . and one of the chief figures, perhaps the very chief, to which this interest attaches itself is St. Francis. And why? Because of the profound popular instinct which enabled him, more than any other man since the primitive age, to fit religion for popular use. . . . He provided the most popular body of ministers of religion that has ever existed in the Church. He transformed monachism by uprooting the stationary monk, delivering him from the bondage of property and sending him as a mendicant friar to be a stranger and sojourner, not in the wilderness, but in the most crowded haunts of men, to console them and to do them good.

MATTHEW ARNOLD
Essays in Criticism

3

Of Holy Poverty

O LOVE of Holy Poverty !
   Thou Kingdom of Tranquillity.

Poverty whose path is safe and clear,
Hath no griefs, nor rancour, sheds no tears,
Nor of robber hands hath any fear,
Tempests cannot trouble Poverty.

Poverty can die in perfect peace ;
Maketh neither will, nor bond, nor lease.
Leaves the world behind, and lies at ease,
And around her strife can never be.

Poverty, High Wisdom deep and sure,
Unsubdued by earth and earthly lure,
Scorns created things, detached and pure,
Scorning, yet pursuing utterly.

He whose wants are master is a slave,
Sells himself for what his longings crave,
Him his purchased riches cannot save,
He hath bargained very foolishly.

Mortal courage sure must hesitate,
Think and turn from such a vassal state,
Where God's image, beautiful and great,
Is debased and changed to vanity.

In a narrow heart God cannot bide :
Where the love is great, the heart is wide ;

3

THE LITTLE BROWN COMPANY

Poverty great-hearted, dignified,
Entertains and welcomes Deity.

Ah! where Christ is grafted on the spray,
All the withered wood is cut away ;
See, the freshness springing from decay !
Changing to a wondrous Unity.

Love, that lives and breathes without Desire,
Wisdom, freed from Thought's consuming fire ;
Will, at one with God, that doth aspire
But to obey Him in simplicity.

Lo, I live ! yet not my self alone ;
I am I, yet am I not mine own ;
And this change, cross-wise obscure, unknown,
—Language cannot tell its mystery.

Poverty hath nothing in her hand,
Nothing craves, in sea, or sky, or land :
Hath the Universe at her command !
Dwelling in the heart of liberty.

JACOPONE DA TODI

(From the translation by
Mrs. THEODORE BECK)

4

How two old men showed the Blessed Francis where he might find the Lady Poverty

AND the Blessed Francis, being come out of the city, made haste to reach a certain field, in which, from afar off, he saw two old men sitting, full of a heavy sorrow, the one of which was saying : To whom shall I look save to some Poor Little Man contrite of Heart and who fears my Words ? And the other : For we brought nothing into this World, and it is certain that we can carry nothing out of it. But having food and a covering to our Bodies, let us be therewith content.

And when the Blessed Francis had come up with them, he said unto them : Tell me, I beseech you, where th Lady Poverty dwells, where she feeds her flock, where she takes her rest at noon, for I languish for the Love of her. But they answered him, saying : O good Brother, we have sat here for a Time, and Times, and half a Time, and have often seen her pass this way, and many were they who sought her. Many were they, once upon a time, who walked in her train, but oft she would return alone and desolate, unadorned by jewels or fine raiment, un-escorted by any following. And she would weep bitterly, saying :

The Sons of my Mother have fought against me. But we did answer and say : Have patience, for the Righteous love thee, and now, O Brother, ascend the great and high Mountain whereon the Lord has placed her. For she dwelleth in the Holy Mountain, because God has loved her more than all the tents of Jacob. Giants have failed to follow her footsteps, and the Eagle to fly to the Summit of her Hill. Poverty is the one thing despised of all men, for it is not found in the land of them that live in delights.

Wherefore she is hid from the Eyes of the Living and the fowls of the air know her not. But God understandeth her way ; He knoweth her Dwelling-place. If therefore, O Brother, thou wouldst ascend unto her, put off the Garments of the Pleasures, and lay aside every weight and the sin which besets thee, for unless thou art free from these trammels, thou canst not attain unto her who is placed at so great a height. But because My Lady is gracious, she is easily seen by those who love her and found by those who seek her. To meditate upon Her, O Brother, is perfect Understanding, and whoso watcheth for her shall speedily be secure. Take with thee trusty Companions that thou may'st profit by their Help in the way, for woe to him that is alone : when he falleth he shall have none to raise him up.

But do you uphold one another.

The Lady Poverty
(Montgomery Carmichael's version)

6

5

Assisi

(EASTER 1915)

MIDWAY the mountain-spur the city clings,
    Firm builded on the slope above the vines
And olives, and the stony bickerings
Of headlong Tescio whose white margin shines
In long, wide rings across the treeful lands :
And over it the frowning castle stands.

And o'er the castle, changing brown and green,
The mighty mass of Mount Subasio,
Cloud-shadow-purpled, sleev'd with dark ravine,
Apparel'd with the last keen dazzling snow,
From clouded crag and cairn flings wide its arms
To nether olives, orchard-fields and farms.

Grey stands the city, lonely and austere,
Stern as a prophet that to penance calls,
Fair in her sternness, full of holy fear—
Close-serried ranks of houses, roofs and walls ;
And over these uplifted towers rise,
Four square to time and all her tyrannies.

The beauty of austerity she wears,
The grace of penance doth enray her brows,
Surely the very mien and form she bears
Of Lady Poverty, the crownèd spouse
Of him who gave his Mother-City fame,
In all the lists that know the Christian name.

7

THE LITTLE BROWN COMPANY

The Prince's daughter is all fair within.
Climb the rough paths, O pilgrim, leave the plains
Until gaunt archway and grey wall thou win,
And reach her shrine by steep and narrow lanes ;
And lo ! the roofs and walls, and windows blaze
With riches past thy telling or thy praise.

So is it with the house of Poverty,
So is it ever with Franciscan joy,
And so with penance must it ever be,
A golden peace enwallèd with annoy,
Drear unto him that gazeth from the plain,
But gladdening all her mountain-shrine who gain.

H. E. G. ROPE

6

The Acolade

HIGH in the dark house of Assisi, Francesco Bernardone slept and dreamed of arms. There came to him in the darkness a vision splendid with swords, patterned after the cross in the Crusading fashion, of spears and shields and helmets hung in a high armoury, all bearing the sacred sign. When he awoke he accepted the dream as a trumpet bidding him to the battlefield, and rushed out to take horse and arms. He delighted in all the exercises of chivalry; and was evidently an accomplished cavalier and fighting man by the tests of the tournament and the camp. He would doubtless at any time have preferred a Christian sort of chivalry; but it seems clear that he was also in a mood which thirsted for glory, though in him that glory would always have been identical with honour. He was not without some vision of that wreath of laurel which Caesar had left for all the Latins. As he rode out to war the great gate in the deep wall of Assisi resounded with his last boast: " I shall come back a great prince."

A little way along his road his sickness rose again and threw him. It seems highly probable, in the light of his impetuous temper, that he had ridden away long before he was fit to move. And in the darkness of this second and far more desolating interruption he seems to have had another dream in which a voice said to him: " You have mistaken the meaning of the vision. Return to your own town." And Francis trailed back in his sickness to Assisi a very dismal and disappointed and perhaps even derided figure, with nothing to do but to wait for what should happen next. It was his first descent into a dark ravine that is called the valley of

9

humiliation, which seemed to him very rocky and desolate, but in which he was afterwards to find many flowers.

But he was not only disappointed and humiliated ; he was also very much puzzled and bewildered. He still firmly believed that his two dreams must have meant something ; and he could not imagine what they could possibly mean. It was while he was drifting, one may even say mooning, about the streets of Assisi and the fields outside the city wall, that an incident occurred to him which has not always been immediately connected with the business of the dreams, but which seems to me the obvious culmination of them. He was riding listlessly in some wayside place, apparently in the open country, when he saw a figure coming along the road towards him and halted ; for he saw it was a leper. And he knew instantly that his courage was challenged, not as the world challenges, but as one would challenge who knew the secrets of the heart of a man. What he saw advancing was not the banners and spears of Perugia, from which it never occurred to him to shrink ; not the armies that fought for the crown of Sicily, of which he had always thought as a courageous man thinks of mere vulgar danger. Francis Bernardone saw his fear coming up the road towards him ; the fear that comes from within and not without ; though it stood white and horrible in the sunlight. For once in the long rush of his life his soul must have stood still. Then he sprang from his horse, knowing nothing between stillness and swiftness, and rushed on the leper and threw his arms round him. It was the beginning of a long vocation of ministry among many lepers, for whom he did many services ; to this man he gave what money he could and mounted and rode on. We do not know how far he rode, or with what sense of the things around him : but it is said that when he looked back he could see no figure on the road.
G. K. CHESTERTON
St. Francis of Assisi

7
Our Lady of the Angels

NOW on this day resounds with holy anthems,
　　Mary's fair house, most dear to blessed Francis,
Which with rich gifts Christ favoured, at the gentle
　　　　Prayer of His mother.

Jesus had promised : mother, what thou askest
That will I grant thee : whoso cometh hither
Mourning his sins, shall here from every vengeance,
　　　　Freely be pardoned.

Wherefore the crowds about the house of Mary,
Circle, and here receive their hoped salvation ;
Here where the entrance of the life eternal
　　　　Stands never closed.

Here from far lands folks hasten with their offerings,
Decking the Virgin's house : their Patron's altar :
Strive in their turn with grateful gifts to load, the
　　　　Men of Assisi.

Soon doth the lowly house whereon Christ's blessing
Resteth, become a temple great and glorious :
Henceforth its fame spreads ever more renowned
　　　　Over the wide world.

Soon on far shores arise a thousand temples,
Whereon the same high favour He bestoweth,
To whom on earth o'er lowly things God giveth
　　　　Power in the highest.

11

THE LITTLE BROWN COMPANY

Praise be forever to the Triune Godhead,
Who, moved to mercy at the prayers of Mary,
Granteth the guilty pardon, and remitteth
    Guilt's fit chastising.

Mirror of Perfection
(Translation by ALAN G. MacDOUGALL)

8

The City of St. Francis

ASSISI is the city of St. Francis. It is impossible to think of anything but his simple and lovely life within the walls of what is really a great, shrunken village, lean and emaciated with years and the ecstacies of the spiritual life. The little town has itself become a Religious and has attained to a profound annihilation in God. Up and down its silent streets wander divine expectancies, a little sad and pessimistic, and yet beautiful withal, because long and long ago Jesus of Nazareth seemed to have returned to His earth. One finds oneself alone with the twelfth and thirteenth centuries and all that they have bequeathed and stored for us within the walls of this softly coloured city, warm with divine love, ruddy with the pale coloured lip of Subasio, from whose side she has, as it were, been hewn with only so simple a rearrangement of the stones as will allow of life, while one contemplates the story of Jesus of Nazareth or St. Francis of Assisi. Hallowed by the tears and the footsteps, sorrowful and bleeding, of many thousands of pilgrims, she has grown lovely under their love, beautiful in some exquisite Christian manner with the sorrows that the world has laid at her feet for hundreds of years now ; a simple country Virgin, very pure and innocent, who had but one lover, Christ her Lord.

EDWARD HUTTON
The Cities of Umbria

13

9

Cloister

"SHOW me your Cloister," asks the Lady
Poverty.

Well, that were a cloister : for its bars
Long strips of sunset ; and its roof the stars.

Four walls of sky, with corridors of air
Leading to chapel, and God everywhere.

Earth beauteous and bare to lie upon,
Lit by the little candle of the sun.

The wind gone daily sweeping like a broom—
For these vast hearts it was a narrow room.

CHARLES L. O'DONNELL, C.S.C.

From " Cloister and other Poems."
Copyright, 1922, by the Macmillan Company.

IO

Of the Sojourn of My Lady Poverty with the Brothers

AND when the Brothers had made all things ready they urged the Lady Poverty to eat with them. But she said unto them : Show me first your Oratory, the Cloister and Chapter House, the Refectory, Kitchen, Dormitory and Stables, your fine Seats and polished Tables and noble Houses. For I see none of these things, and yet I do see that you are blithe and cheerful, abounding in Joy, filled with Consolation, as if you expected all these things to be supplied to you at will.

But they made answer and said : O Lady and Queen, we thy servants are weary with the long journey, and thou in coming with us hast endured not a little. Therefore, if it please thee, let us eat first, and thus refreshed, we will do thy Bidding. And my Lady answered : It pleaseth me well. But first bring Water that we wash our Hands and a Cloth wherewith to dry them. And they brought forth a broken earthenware Vessel—for they had no sound one—full of Water. And having poured the Water on her hands they searched on all sides for a Cloth. But when none could be found, one of the Brethren offered the Habit he wore, that therewith my Lady might wipe her hands. And giving Thanks she took it, magnifying God with all her Heart Who had given her such Men as Companions. And after this they led her to the Place where the Table was made ready. But she looked round about, and seeing nothing save three or four crusts of Barley-bread laid upon the Grass, she

15

marvelled exceedingly within herself, saying : Who ever saw the like in the Generations of Old. Blessed art Thou, O Lord God, Who hast care of All, for Thy Power is at hand when Thou wilt,—Thou hast taught Thy people that by such works they may please Thee. And thus they sat a while giving thanks to God for all His Gifts. Then my Lady Poverty commanded them to bring in dishes the Food which they had cooked. But they fetched a Basin of cold Water, that all might dip their Bread therein, for there was no abundance of Dishes or Superfluity of Cooks. My Lady Poverty then begged that she might at least have some uncooked Herbs, but having neither Garden nor Gardener the Brethren gathered some wild Herbs in the Wood, and placed them before her. Who said : Bring me a little Salt, that I may savour these Herbs, for they are bitter. But they answered her : Then must Thou tarry a while, Lady, until we go into the City to obtain it, if haply there should be any one who would give us some. Then she asked them, saying : Fetch hither a Knife that I may trim these Herbs, and cut the Bread, which verily is hard and dry. Who answered : O Lady, we have no Smith to make us a Knife. For the present use thy Teeth in the place of a Knife and afterwards we will provide. Whereupon she said : Have you a little Wine ? To which they answered: No, Lady, we have no Wine, for the necessaries of Man's Life are Bread and Water, and it is not good for thee to drink Wine, for the Spouse of Christ should shun Wine as Poison. And when they were satisfied, rejoicing more in the Nobility of Want than if they had an Abundance of All things, they blessed the Lord in Whose Sight they had found such Favour and led my Lady Poverty to a place where she might sleep, for she was weary. And she lay down upon the bare ground. And when she asked for a Pillow, they straightway brought her a Stone, and laid it under her Head. So after she had slept for a brief space in Peace, she arose and asked the Brothers to show her their Cloister. And they, leading her to the Summit of a Hill, showed her the wide World, saying : " This is our Cloister, O Lady Poverty." Thereupon she bade them all sit down together, and opening her mouth she began to speak unto them Words of Life. . . .

The Lady Poverty
(MONTGOMERY CARMICHAEL'S version)

II

St. Francis to the Birds

LITTLE sisters the birds ;
   We must praise God, you and I—
You with songs that fill the sky,
I, with halting words.

All things tell His praise,
Woods and waters thereof sing,
Summer, Winter, Autumn, Spring,
And the nights and days.

Yea, and cold and heat,
And the sun and stars and moon,
Sea with her monotonous tune,
Rain and hail and sleet.

And the winds of heaven,
And the solemn hills of blue,
And the brown earth and the dew,
And the thunder, even.

And the flower's sweet breath.
All things make one glorious voice ;
Life with fleeting pains and joys,
And our sister Death.

Little flowers of air,
With your feathers soft and sleek
And your bright brown eyes and meek
He hath made you fair.

18

THE LITTLE BROWN COMPANY

He hath taught to you
Skill to weave in tree and thatch
Nests where happy mothers hatch
Speckled eggs of blue.

And hath children given :
When the soft heads overbrim
The brown nests, then thank ye Him
In the clouds of heaven.

Also in your lives
Live His laws Who loveth you,
Husbands, be ye kind and true ;
Be home-keeping, wives.

Love not gossiping ;
Stay at home and keep the nest ;
Fly not here and there in quest
Of the newest thing.

Live as brethren live :
Love be in each heart and mouth ;
Be not envious, be not wroth,
Be not slow to give.

When ye build the nest,
Quarrel not o'er straw or wool ;
He who hath be bountiful
To the neediest.

Be not puffed nor vain
Of your beauty or your worth,
Of your children or your birth,
Or the praise you gain.

Eat not greedily :
Sometimes for sweet mercy's sake

THE LITTLE BROWN COMPANY

Worm or insect spare to take :
Let it crawl or fly.

See ye sing not near
To our church on holy day,
Lest the human folk should stray
From their prayers to hear.

Now depart in peace :
In God's name I bless each one ;
May your days be long i' the sun
And your joys increase.

And remember me,
Your poor brother Francis, who
Loves you and gives thanks to you
For this courtesy.

Sometimes when ye sing,
Name my name that He may take
Pity for the dear song's sake
On my shortcomings.

KATHARINE TYNAN HINKSON

12

How St. Francis taught Brother Leo how to answer him, and the Brother could not say anything, but the contrary of what St. Francis desired

ONCE on a time, in the beginning of the Order, St. Francis was lodged with Brother Leo in a place where there were no books to say the divine Office with. And when the hour came for matins St. Francis said to Brother Leo :

" My beloved, we have no breviary with which to say matins, but in order that we may spend the time praising God, I will speak, and thou shalt answer me as I shall instruct thee, and take heed that thou say not a word other than as I tell thee.   I will say thus :

'O Brother Francis, thou hast done so many evils and so many sins in thy time, that thou hast merited hell :'

And thou, Brother Leo, shalt answer :

'Truly, and thou dost merit the deepest hell.' "

And Brother Leo, with the simplicity of a little dove, replied : " Willingly, Father ; begin in the name of God."

Then St. Francis began to say :

" O Brother Francis, thou hast done so many evils and so many sins in thy time, that thou has merited hell."

And Brother Leo replied :

" God will work so much good through thee that thou shalt go to Paradise."   Then said St. Francis :

" Say not thus, Brother Leo, but when I shall say :

'Brother Francis, thou hast committed so many

21

iniquities against God, that thou art worthy to be accursed of God,' do thou answer thus :

'Verily thou art worthy to be placed among the accursed.' "

And Brother Leo replied : " Willingly, Father."

Again St. Francis with many tears and sighs, beating his breast, said with a loud voice : " O my Lord, Lord of heaven and earth, I have committed against Thee so many iniquities and so many grievous sins that I am worthy to be accursed of Thee for them all." And Brother Leo replied : " O Brother Francis, God will make thee such, that among the blessed thou shalt be singularly blessed."

And St. Francis, marvelling that Brother Leo answered contrariwise to what he had imposed on him, reproved him, saying : " Wherefore dost thou not answer as I instructed thee ? I command thee, by holy obedience, to answer as I will tell thee. I will speak thus :

' O Brother Francis, thou little wicked one, dost thou think that God will have mercy on thee, knowing that thou hast committed so many sins against the God of mercy, and God of all consolations, that thou art not worthy to find mercy ?' And thou, Brother Leo, little sheep, shalt answer : ' By no means are thou worthy to find mercy.' "

But when St. Francis said : " O Brother Francis, thou wicked one," and the rest, Brother Leo answered him :

" God the Father, whose mercy is infinitely more than thy sins, will show thee great mercy, and more than this, will add to thee many graces."

At which reply, St. Francis, gently angry and patiently wrath, said to Brother Leo : " And wherefore hast thou presumed to act contrary to obedience, and so many times answered contrary to what I imposed on thee ? "

Brother Leo replied humbly and reverently :

" God knows, my Father, that each time I had it in my heart to answer as thou hadst commanded me, but

God makes me speak as it pleases Him, not as it pleases me."

At which St. Francis marvelled, and said to Brother Leo : " I pray thee from my heart that this time thou wilt answer as I have told thee."

And Brother Leo answered : " I speak in the name of God, for this time I will answer as thou desirest."

And St. Francis said, weeping : " O Brother Francis, thou little wicked one, dost thou think God will have mercy on thee ? "

Brother Leo replied : " Yea, rather thou shalt receive great graces from God, and He will exalt thee, and glorify thee to all eternity, because he that humbleth himself shall be exalted, and I cannot say otherwise, for God speaks by my mouth." And in this humble contention, with many tears and much spiritual consolation, they continued till the end of the day.

The Fioretta

13

The Mendicant

A GHOSTLY rogue and vagabond
    I foot the upland track,
Nor bide behind one cloister wall
But beg an alms of each and all
To carry in my pack.

My habit 'tis the beggar's cloak
Whereat men merry make—
A patch of grey, a patch of brown,
The motley of a monarch's clown
Worn gaily for His sake.

Of Benedict his sons I beg
A maxim for my day.
Where Carmel sounds her stintless psalms
I crave a spiritual alms
To sing me on my way.

At sweet St. Bridget's board I'm fed
When on her door I knock ;
I share the Servites' broken bread,
And find a pillow for my head
Where Philip folds his flock.

Ignatius speeds me on my road
With nectar from his bowl,
The cheer of Bernard wings my feet
And Dominic and Francis meet
And mingle in their dole.

24

THE LITTLE BROWN COMPANY

To beg my spirit's livelihood
I've paused at every gate—
At every hostel of the Rood
As " Brother Nobody " pursued
My soul's novitiate.

And now, when these my motley rags
The passing pilgrims scan,
Whate'er their scrip, whate'er their sign,
Their hearts cry gladly, greeting mine,
" Hail ! Brother Everyman ! "

ENID DINNIS

14

The Joyous Penitents

THE first brothers lived as did the poor people among whom they so willingly moved ; Portiuncula was their favourite church, but it would be a mistake to suppose that they sojourned there for any long period. It was their place of meeting, nothing more. When they set forth they simply knew that they should meet again in the neighbourhood of the modest chapel. Their life was that of the Umbrian beggars of the present day, going here and there as fancy dictated, sleeping in haylofts, in leper hospitals or under the porch of some church. So little had they any fixed abode that Egidio, having decided to join them, was at considerable trouble to find Francis, and accidentally meeting him in the neighbourhood of Rivo Torto, he saw in the fact a providential leading. They went up and down the country, joyfully sowing their seed. It was the beginning of summer, the time when everybody in Umbria is out of doors mowing or turning the grass. The customs of the country have changed but little. Walking, in the end of May, in the fields about Florence, Perugia or Rieta, one still sees at nightfall the bagpipers entering the fields as the mowers seat themselves upon the haycocks for their evening meal. They play a few pieces and then the train of haymakers return to the village followed by the harvest-laden carts. It is they who lead the procession, rending the air with their sharpest strains. The Joyous Penitents, who loved to call themselves *Joculatores Domini*, God's jongleurs, no doubt often did the same. They did even better, for not willing to be a charge to any one, they passed a part of the

26

day in aiding the peasants in their field-work. The inhabitants of these districts are for the most part kindly and sedate. The Friars soon gained their confidence by relating to them first their history and then their hopes. They worked and ate together, field-hands and Friars, often slept in the same barn, and when with the morrow's dawn the Friars went on their way, the hearts of those they left behind had been touched. They were not yet converted, but they knew that not far away, over towards Assisi, were living men who had renounced all worldly goods and who, consumed with zeal, were going up and down preaching penitence and peace.

PAUL SABATIER
Life of St. Francis

27

15
The Lady Poverty

THE Lady Poverty was fair :
    But she has lost her looks of late,
With change of times and change of air.
Ah slattern ! she neglects her hair,
Her gown, her shoes ; she keeps no state
As once when her pure feet were bare.

Or—almost worse, if worse can be—
She scolds in parlours, dusts and trims,
Watches and counts, O is this she
Whom Francis met, whose step was free,
Who with obedience carolled hymns,
In Umbria walked with Chastity ?

Where is her ladyhood ?   Not here,
Not among modern kinds of men ;
But in the stony fields where clear
Through the thin trees the skies appear
In delicate spare soil and fen,
And slender landscape and austere.

                                    ALICE MEYNELL

16

The Sacramental Sign

THE Franciscan life can no more be set down in terms of speech than can Christianity itself. It escapes words, and can only be embodied in a living tradition. If, as is commonly the case, we sum up the ideal of the Order in the word " Poverty," we leave unexpressed other aspects, such as simplicity of soul, love of one's neighbour and joyousness, all which enter into the ideal of the Franciscan life quite as much as poverty. In truth Franciscan poverty is but the symbol or sacramental sign of that many-sided life which is included in the following of Christ in His redemptive mission to men. And in this it differs essentially from the programme of poverty proclaimed by the sectaries of the twelfth and thirteenth centuries . . . with the Friars, poverty represented primarily a personal conversion to Christ ; with the sectaries it was a political programme.[1]

It is evident that this Franciscan poverty in its simplest form, as embraced by Francis and his fraternity, would be unworkable in the ordinary life of the world. Nor did Francis himself ever consider it as applicable to society at large. Even to his lay followers, or tertiaries as they are now called, he handed it on only in a modified form. With them it was to be a spiritual leaven in daily life rather than as a hard and fast external rule. At the same time, idealism is always to be tested by its capacity to influence the matter-of-fact life of the multitude ; unless it can do this it is lacking in reality. . . . But it must be remembered that Francis was not directly concerned with

[1] *The Friars and How They Came to England.*

29

the spiritual problem of wealth, but with the spiritual value of poverty as a condition for the realization of the soul's freedom. Others before Francis had shown how wealth and property can be instruments for the upbuilding of Christian character and Christian society. It was Francis who most clearly convinced men that poverty, too, may be a factor in moral and spiritual development.[2]

FATHER CUTHBERT, O.S.F.C.

[2] *The Romanticism of St. Francis.*

17

Our Lord Christ : of order

SET love in order, thou that lovest me,
   Never was virtue out of order found ;
And though I fill thy heart desirously,
By thine own virtue I must keep My ground ;
When to My love thou dost bring charity ;
Even she must come with order girt and gown'd,
Look how the trees are bound
To order, bearing fruit ;
And by one thing compute,
In all things earthly order's grace or gain.

All earthly things I had the making of
Were number'd and were measured then by Me ;
And each was order'd to its end by Love,
Each kept, through order, clean for ministry.
Charity most of all, when known enough,
Is of her very nature orderly.
Lo, now ! what heat in thee,
Soul, can have bred this rout ?
Thou putt'st all order out,
Even this love's heat must be its curb and rein.

                   St. Francis
           (D. G. ROSSETTI's version)

18

The Golden Sayings of Brother Giles

NO man can come to the knowledge of God except by humility.

What is humility ? Give each his due.

If thou wilt know much, labour much and bow thy head much.

Man fashioneth God as he desireth ; but He is always such as He is.

Any one who honours others can hardly ever fall grievously.

The devil does not despair of a man so long as he seeth him to have flesh.

What a mass of water the river Tiber would hold if it were not continually flowing.

Blessed is he who judgeth himself now, for he will not come to another judgment.

Blessed is he who loveth and doth not therefore desire to be loved ; blessed is he who feareth and does not therefore desire to be feared ; blessed is he who serveth and doth not therefore desire to be served ; blessed is he who behaveth well towards others and doth not desire that others behave well towards him ; and because these are great things the foolish do not rise to them.

It is a thousand times better that a man should teach himself than teach the whole world.

THE LITTLE BROWN COMPANY

All that can be thought of, seen, told and touched is nothing in respect to what can neither be thought of, told, seen nor touched.

He who doth not wish to honour others shall not be honoured, and he who doth not wish to know shall not be known, and he who doth not wish to bear fatigue shall not rest.

The devil fleeth from the creature for nothing else than for love. Wherefore a man ought not to rest until he loveth.

If thou workest the good which thou knowest, thou shalt come to the good which thou knowest not.

From the version by
Father Paschal Robinson, O.F.M.

c   33

19
St. Francis and Perfect Joy

BLESSED Saint Francis in the Winter time,
  When half the Umbrian vales were white with snow
And all the northward vine-stems rough with rime,
  Walked from Perugia down. His steps were slow,
Made slow by thought, yet swift at times, for love
  Showered o'er his musings, fired them from above.

Love perfect made, lives in the Loved alone ;
  All gifts by him unshared it spurns as dross ;
He who for earth's sake left His heavenly throne
  From earth accepted one sole gift—the Cross :
That day St. Francis on that Cross and Him
  Mused ever as he walked, with eyes tear-dim.

At last thus spake he to that Brother meek
  For hours sole comrade of his silent way :
" Leone, lamb of Christ, the words I speak
  Write down and ponder over some far-off day ;
For truth remains, but men are winds that pass
  Like those brief gusts that bend yon stiffening grass.

" Leone, we the least of men have striven
  An Order to uprear of Orders least ;
If God, who ofttimes from his feast hath driven
  The proud, and shared Himself the beggar's feast,
Should dower that new-born Order with much grace
  That one day it shall stand the first in place ;

" If in each land the Brothers Minor shone
  Resplendent with a sanctity so high

34

That all men thronged to hear their word and none
   Who heard in mortal sin was known to die,
All crowns of earth to this were but a toy ;
   Yet write that this would not be Perfect Joy."

Another mile that road ice-filmed they trod
   While sank the sun and 'gainst their faces blew
Bitterer the blast, then stood the man of God
   And thus with kindling cheek began anew :
" Leone, little lamb of Christ, attend !
   Write down my words, and inly apprehend.

" Leone, if through all the earth in fear
   Before the Brothers Minor demons fled ;
If in all lands they caused the deaf to hear,
   The blind to see, and raised the buried dead,
All this though greatness proof 'gainst Time's alloy
   And clear from strain would not be Perfect Joy."

When three times now Leone thus had heard
   From lips so loved the selfsame oracle
He stood in wide-eyed wonder without word ;
   At last he spake : " I pray thee, Father, tell
What thing is Perfect Joy : how won ? where found ?
   In heaven do Angels share it with the Crowned ? "

Blessed Saint Francis raised his thin, small hand
   And pointed to a Chapel now not far
That lonely rose amid the dusking land
   Backed by the dull red sky and evening star ;
Scarce larger than a huge tree's hollow hole
   That Chapel seemed, their daylong journey's goal.

Thus spake the Saint : " Leone, see'st thou there
   Our happy home ?   If we who left it late
So bright, so glad, so silent, and so fair
   Should cower snow-clad ere compline by its gate,

And sue admittance crying, ' Porter, wake'!
  Receive thy Brethren for the Master's sake.'

" And if that porter loth to leave his bed,
  Should answer from within, ' Imposters base !
Come ye to gorge the olives and the bread
  Reserved for orphans and the sick ? give place !
This knotted staff for backs like yours were blest ;
  Hence !   Psalms are over, and the Brethren rest.'

" And if, an hour gone by, once more we came
  And prayed : ' Great Sir, unbar to us the door ;
Two Brothers Minor spent, thy pity claim,
  Wanderers wayworn, heart weary, and footsore ' :
And he made answer : ' Hence ! for, though I sleep,
  For bandits masked my wolf-hounds vigil keep.'

" And, if two hours gone by, again we sued
  And forth that porter rushed with staff and hound,
Doubtless not knowing us in his Cain-like mood,
  And left us on the snows bleeding and bound
Till now on the blank road the morning shone,
  And we at heart had cherished petulance none,

" Nor uttered contumelious word the while,
  But mused all night in Christ and on his Cross,
And thanked Him that he deigned with us, though vile,
  To share it, gain supreme disguised in loss,
And endless bliss won by an hour's annoy,
  Leone, Brother, that were Perfect Joy.

" Leone, that and every grace beside,
  Is gift of God to nought man boasts akin ;
Great sin it were to turn God's gifts to pride :—
  This gift, slaying self love, forestall such sin ! "
Well, cried the Apostle, pain-emparadised,
  " Glory, in this I will—the Cross of Christ."

                       AUBREY DE VERE

20

Renunciation

(WRITTEN AT ASSISI, April 15, 1874)

BUT thirty years ago I knew once or twice what joy meant, and have not forgotten the feeling ; nay, even so little a while as two years ago, I had it back again for a day. And I can assure you, good Wiseacres, there is such a thing to be had ; but not in cheap shops, nor, I was going to say, for money ; yet in a certain sense it is buyable—by forsaking all that a man hath. Buyable, literally enough—the freehold Elysian fixed at that price, but not a doit cheaper ; and I believe, at this moment, the reason my voice has an uncertain sound, the reason that this design of mine stays unhelped, and that only a little group of men and women, moved chiefly by personal regard, stand with me in a course so plain and true, is that I have not yet given myself to it wholly, but have halted between good and evil, and sit still at the receipt of custom, and am always looking back from the plough. It is not wholly my fault this. There seems to me good reasons why I should go on with my work at Oxford ; good reasons why I should make myself as comfortable as I can wherever I go ; travel with two servants and have a dish of game at dinner. It seems to me that I have given the half of my foods and more to the poor ; it is true also that my work in Oxford is not a matter of pride, but of duty with me ; it is true that I think it wise to live what seems to other people a rational and pleasant, not an enthusiastic life, and that I serve my servants at least as much as they serve me. But, all this being so, I find

37

there is yet something wrong. I have no peace, much less ecstasy. It seems to me as if one had indeed to wear camel's hair instead of dress coats before one can get that ; and I was looking at St. Francis's camel's-hair coat yesterday (they have it still in the sacristy), and I don't like the look of it at all.

JOHN RUSKIN
Fors Clavigera, Letter XLI

21

Cor Dulce

THROUGH Umbria when the dear St. Francis went,
　　Preaching in many a hamlet, many a town—
Oh, sweet St. Francis in his faded gown ;
His eyes on fire, his curved lips innocent !—
Often he fell to weeping bitterly,
With cries, and sobs, and tears uncomforted ;
And still " O Love unloved ! " made all his cry ;
" O Love that goes unloved ! " was all he said.

O Love unloved ! I have a Lover true,
Whose love exceedeth all the loves that be ;
O mine own Lover, yet unloved of me,
My Love who loved me in old years and new !
Waiting for me beneath the midnight skies,
With thorns, and blood, and death-dews on His head.
And pierced entreating hands, and yearning eyes :
Who loved me still when other loves were fled.

If such a love were given to you, or you—
A love that sought you in the throes of death,
That thirsted for you with its dying breath,
Yea, held death sweet that was endured for you,
Embraced the Cross that broke it for your sake :—
I wonder would your recompense be this :
To give Him gall His dying thirst to slake,
To kiss Him, and betray Him with your kiss !

And I who was His chosen and His bride,
Sat at His feast, and drank the selfsame cup,

39

THE LITTLE BROWN COMPANY

Dipped in the dish with Him when He did sup ;
Then left Him and went out in the night-tide,
And so betrayed Him to His enemies,
Yea, and did smite Him who hath loved so well.
Say, friends, and how shall I atone for this,
And purge me from my guilt intolerable.

Ah me, ah me !   I dare not lift mine eyes,
Who may again betray Him ere night goes ;
Who may deny Him ere the shrill cock crows.
O happy thief who hath His paradise,
Why do I turn to thoughts of you to-day ;
And meek St. Peter, who sinned heavily,
Yet washed with lifelong tears his guilt away ;
Rather than all the sinless saints that be ?

O Love unloved, my Love that goes unloved !
For all your Passion's sake, your lonely grave,
For that unstinted wealth of love you gave ;
O Love unloved, sweet Love that loves unloved !
Break me, a reed, or bind me who are strong,
And make me strong to suffer and resist,
And give me tears to weep a whole life long,
The traitor's kiss wherewith your face was kissed !

KATHARINE TYNAN HINKSON

22

The Vision Splendid

NEVER be misled by modern writers into thinking
that the Catholic Church behaved badly to Francis;
the Catholic Church behaved gloriously to Francis.
Realize how convincing the goodness of Francis must
have been, and what sincere goodness must have met him
in the person of Pope Innocent III. for this to have been
possible, for Francis was not a trim and sober-looking
monk, remember, the scornful would have said he was a
cracked young man dressed in corduroys and a smock
frock. When Assisi found that the Holy Father had
given Francis leave to go on, it began to consider the
whole thing with increased seriousness, and to take
some anxious motherly pride in these delightful per-
plexing men ; but it took longer for the country folk
to change their minds, and the little brothers, now more
laughing and confident than ever, continued to have rough
experiences.

They had all settled down for a time in a disused barn
at a place called Rivo Torto, which means " the winding
stream," out of sight of Assisi. Here the new-comers
learned the hard lesson of poverty.

Think of a cold, wet day in the old barn, two brothers
have gone to beg, nobody knows whether there will be
enough for supper ; there is no fire, there are no books
to read, no chairs to sit on, and the rain is coming in
through the roof and making puddles on the ground.
And then think of Oxford as you have seen it from the
top of Magdalen Tower. The inspiration which built
what you see was kindled by the fact that those men

endured wet weather in that leaky barn. For St. Dominic took his poverty from St. Francis, and it was the religion of St. Francis and St. Dominic which built Oxford.

REV. H. F. B. MACKAY
The Message of Francis of Assisi

23

Brother Ass and St. Francis

IT came to pass
    That " Brother Ass "
(As he his Body named),
Unto the Saint
Thus made complaint :
" I am unjustly blamed.

" Whate'er I do,
Like Balaam you
Requite me with a blow,
As for offence
To recompense
An ignominious foe.

" God made us one,
And I have done
No wickedness alone ;
Nor can I do
Apart from you,
An evil all my own.

" If Passion stir,
'Tis you that spur
My frenzy to the goal :
Then be the blame
Where sits the shame,
Upon the goading soul.

" Should one or both
Be blind or loth

THE LITTLE BROWN COMPANY

Our brotherhood to see,
Remember this,
You needs must miss
Or enter heaven through *me*."

To this complaint
The lowly Saint
In tears replied, " Alas,
If so it be,
God punish me
And bless thee, Brother Ass."

J. B. TABB

24

St. Francis' Salutation of the Virtues

HAIL, queen wisdom ! May the Lord save thee with thy sister holy pure simplicity !

O Lady, holy poverty, may the Lord save thee with thy sister holy humility !

O Lady, holy charity, may the Lord save thee with thy sister holy obedience !

O all ye most holy virtues, may the Lord from whom you proceed and come, save you !

There is absolutely no man in the whole world who can possess one among you unless he first die. He who possesses one, and does not offend the others, possesses all ; and he who offends one, possesses none and offends all ; and every one (of them) confounds vices and sins. Holy wisdom confounds Satan and all his wickedness. Pure holy simplicity confounds all the wisdom of this world and the wisdom of the flesh. Holy poverty confounds cupidity and avarice and the cares of this world. Holy humility confounds pride and all the men of this world and all things that are in the world. Holy charity confounds all diabolical and fleshly temptations and all fleshly fears. Holy obedience confounds all bodily and fleshly desires and keeps the body mortified to the obedience of the spirit and to the obedience of one's brother, and makes a man subject to all the men of this world and not to men alone, but also to all beasts and wild animals, so that they may do with him whatsoever they will, in so far as it may be granted to them from above by the Lord.

From the version by
FATHER PASCHAL ROBINSON, O.F.M.
45

25

The Ascent

THEY who have passed before
   Unto the higher mountain, and no more
Breast at our sides the slopes that touch the plain—
Between us loom
The craggy shoulders of the frowning edge,
Yet downward thro' the shadow'd gloom
Come songs of gladness from the half-seen ridge :
And ever and again—
Little glimpses of hill-cities swath'd in rain ;
Like Monticelio and Saint Angelo
That sudden waves of sunlight oversweep
And sudden clouds o'erblow
Beneath Genaro's swarthy steep,—
Their buoyant forms are seen
In storm and starlight keen,
Their voices raise
A sudden thunderpeal of praise.
And ever and anon
They hail us on :
" Heed thou no subtle fears : "
Lighter and fuller hence appears
The outstretch of the unreturning years.
Fear not to lose
Their so-grudged treasures, nor refuse
The instant answer to the challenge, " Choose ! "
Choose God in all.
Finally, firmly, boldly, once for all.
And thou shalt in thine own soul verify
The hundredfold

46

THE LITTLE BROWN COMPANY

Eternal Truth hath promised thee of old,
And Faith, well-nigh
Grown sight, must needs outcall
Franciscanly
" My God ! My All ! "

H. E. G. ROPE

26

How Brother Fire dealt gently with God's Servant

AND although he had attained to great purity of mind and body he ceased not—regardless of the danger to his bodily health—to purify his mental sight by continual tears. Now, by this constant weeping he brought on a grievous malady in his eyes, and the physicians would have persuaded him to restrain his tears : but the Blessed Francis replied : " It is not fitting, Brother Physician, that for the love of that light which we have here below, in common with the flies, we should shut out the least ray of the eternal light which visits us from above : for the soul has not received the light for the sake of the body, but the body for the sake of the soul. I would, therefore, choose rather to lose the light of the body than to repress those tears by which the interior eyes are purified, that so they may see God, lest I should thus quench the spirit of devotion."

Having been often counselled by the physicians, and also earnestly besought by the brethren to suffer the application of a cautery for the relief of his eyes, the man of God humbly assented, seeing that the remedy would be at once salutary and painful. The surgeon was therefore sent for, who placed the iron instrument in the fire. The servant consoled his shuddering body, as if it had been a friend, saying to the fire : " O brother fire, the Most High has created thee glorious, mighty, beautiful, and useful above all other creatures. Be thou propitious and healthful to me at this hour. I beseech the great Lord

Who created thee, so sweetly to temper thy heat that I may be able to endure it."

When he had finished his prayers he made the sign of the Cross upon the red iron and firmly waited its touch. Then was the seething iron driven deep into the tender flesh, making a deep gash from the ear to the eyebrow. When he was asked concerning the pain caused by the fire, the holy man made answer : " Praise the Most High, my brethren, for I tell you truly that I have neither felt nor suffered from the burning iron " ; and, turning to the surgeon, he said : " If the flesh is not sufficiently burnt, burn it again." And the surgeon when he beheld the might of the spirit in the weakness of the flesh, marvelled greatly, and extolled that divine miracle, saying : " I tell you, brothers, I have seen wonders to-day."

The man of God had attained to such a degree of purity that his flesh was subject to his spirit, and his spirit to God in a wonderful harmony and agreement, and all creatures were thus in marvellous subjection to his will and command, who was himself the faithful servant of the Creator.

Legenda St. Bonaventure
(Miss Lockhart's Version)

27

A Portrait

OH, Poverello, sweetest, mildest Saint !
　　How well I note thy meekness while I paint,
With careful brush the candour of thine eyes ;
But I grow sad and unbidden tears arise—
Thy lips are all too gentle for my brush,
They seem some softest petal that I crush ;
For painting them as they should be
Is, ah ! too great an art for me.

Thine eyes, thy head and hands, thy sandalled feet,
All speak to me of sacrifice complete ;
That peasant garb, that little poorest cord
For poverty's sweet sustenance implored.
Poor little one of Christ, while thou dost stand
Thus poor, I see great treasure in thy hand,
All gleaming ruddy 'mid each palm,
As round thee glows God's peace, sweet and calm.

My brushes droop, their work is done ;
My own defeat " poor little one."
Yet have they taught my soul to love
More than I guessed their art could prove ;
Thy portrait in my soul must shine ;
Assisi's saint—all men's—and mine.

NANCY DUSTAN

28
The Portrait of St. Francis

WE have lost the portrait which according to one biographer was painted in 1212 by a certain Melorinus. But another has come down to us which dates from about ten years later and which is to be seen on a pillar of a small chapel in the Benedictine convent at Subiaco. St. Francis is there represented standing, with bare feet, and holding a paper on which these words are written, " Peace be to this house." He has neither nimbus nor stigmata, and the inscription describes him simply as Brother Francis, without any allusion to his being a saint or any indication of his canonization. All this points to its having been painted in 1222, two years before Alvernia and four years before his death, during the Retreat which the Saint wished to make in the first hermitage of his great predecessor and model, the father of the monastic life, St. Benedict of Norcia. The painter, according to M. Thode, was in all probability a student and contemporary of the Roman master, Conxolus, who painted and signed a Madonna in the lower church at Subiaco. . . .

There are other portraits of St. Francis almost as old and certainly as genuine as the fresco at Subiaco. One is at Rome in the Church of St. Francis a Ripa, and a venerable tradition has it that it belonged to a noble lady who was a great friend of the Saint, Jaqueline of Settesoli, she whom he used to call " Brother Jaqueline." A touching picture in the baptistry at Parma depicts under a strange and grandiose form the scene at Alvernia, the ecstasy of the Saint and the cherubim. There is a signed portrait by Berlinghieri, dated 1235, in the Church of St. Francis at Pescia ; an anonymous portrait at the convent at Greccio, in which the Saint is represented sobbing and wiping away his tears. All these pictures remain fairly close to the one at Subiaco ; it is always the same long oval face, with delicate and clear-cut features, and with the thin beard about the cheeks and chin.

But a different type soon began to appear in a number of later portraits. They are to be found in the Vatican and in the Franciscan Convent of Our Lady of the Angels. The features begin to harden, the cheeks grow hollow, the eyes become larger and sunken ; the whole face becomes more bony and bears the mark of a repellent asceticism. The indefinable refinement, courtesy and lovableness which proclaimed in the beggar the man of the world and the nobleman and which pierces so appealingly the coarse habit of the fresco at Subiaco is purposely kept out of the picture. Nothing but a rugged and almost repulsive type of austerity remains. These are undoubtedly paintings due to the influence of the Spirituals and those of the extreme left of the Franciscan Order. The same exaggeration and taste for the deformity produced by torment can be recognised in them as in the Christs of Giunta of Pisa and Cimabue.

That is the Franciscan type already debased and arbitrary, a mannered type robbed of all its grace and original sweetness, meant to edify, which was popularised towards the middle of the thirteenth century in the host of portraits which eventually succeeded in becoming authoritative. . . . As a contrast to this Florentine type, simplified and disfigured, it is curious to note the entirely different tradition adopted subsequently by the Sienese school of painting. At the Academy of Siena is to be seen a picture by an anonymous artist which has been reproduced by Wizewa in his translation of the *St. Francis* of Jörgensen.

THE LITTLE BROWN COMPANY

Following a custom in vogue in his day for altarpieces, the artist has arranged around his principal figure two columns of little scenes, about the size of a miniature, representing episodes in the life of his hero. These small vignettes are assuredly masterpieces of Franciscan religious painting. Never has the touching and veridical legend been painted with more freshness and poetry. As for the picture of the Saint itself, the artist of Siena, by an exquisite gift of second sight, has made it a type of refined and chivalrous beauty, an aristocratic presentment both human and devotional. This remained the model for the whole school of Siena. It is the most lifelike since the original portrait and one which radiates the best, after the portrait at Subiaco, the rich nobility and supernatural charm of the well-beloved Saint of Assisi.

Louis Gillet
(From a lecture on " The Franciscan
Influence on Art ")

*   *   *   *   *   *

29

IN stature he was a little above the middle size ; his head was round and not too large ; his face was oval and his features drawn ; his forehead was small and even ; his eyes were of medium size, black and truthful ; black hair, eyebrows straight, a nose fine, even and straight, ears erect and small, and flat temples constituted the upper part of his countenance ; his voice was vehement, sweet, clear and sonorous ; his teeth were closely set, even, white, his lips small and thin ; his slender neck was set on square shoulders, and his short arms ended in small hands with long fingers, the nails of which were projecting ; his legs were slender and his feet small ; his skin was thin and he was very lean ; he was coarse in his attire,

53

THE LITTLE BROWN COMPANY

he slept little, and gave abundantly of the little he had ; because he was most humble, he showed himself mild to all, and conforming himself to the customs of others he surpassed the most holy in Sanctity, and when among sinners considered himself one of them.

THOMAS OF CELANO

54

30

Sorrow

OF Sorrow, 'tis as Saints have said—
    That his ill-savoured lamp shall shed
A light to Heaven ; when blown about
    By the world's vain and windy rout,
The candles of delight burn out.

Then usher Sorrow to thy board,
    Give him such fire as may afford
Thy single habitation—best
    To meet him half-way in his quest,
The importunate and sad-eyed guest.

Yet somewhat should he give who took
    Thy hospitality, for look,
His is no vain vagrancy,
    Beneath his rags what hints there be
Of a celestial livery.

Sweet Sorrow, play a grateful part,
    Break me the marble of my heart
And of its fragments pave a street
    Where, to my bliss, myself may meet
One hastening with piercèd feet.

HELEN PARRY EDEN

31
The Right to be Poor

CHRISTIAN social justice implies the right of an adequate wage and the relief of the poor ; but it also implies the right of the poor to be poor without moral or spiritual degradation. Poverty is one of the liberties of the children of God ; but the world has done its best to destroy that liberty by loading it with conditions which depress the spirit and make for moral and spiritual squalor. The first of these conditions has been the isolation of the poor in the struggle for the necessities of existence. They have been herded into their own dens and narrow quarters, and fenced round with the silent indifference of an outer world. That lack of a wider human fellowship has done more to depress the souls of the poor than any mere economic factor. It has tended to cut them off from interests not connected with their own struggle to live : and mentally and morally as well as physically, has confined them within stifling walls : whereas the natural heritage of the poor, as of all human beings, are the broad highways of human life with their immediate opportunities for the exercise of the soul's faculties. But individual and class selfishness have deprived poverty of this freedom and cramped its spiritual life, too frequently almost to extinction. The poor therefore need freedom ; not so much political freedom, which after all is but a means to an end, and not always a certain means, but the freedom to live properly human lives.

Chiefly they need the freedom of human fellowship.

FATHER CUTHBERT, O.S.F.C.

56

32
The Sermon of St. Francis

UP soared the lark into the air,
  A shaft of song, a winged prayer,
As if a soul, released from pain,
Were flying back to heaven again.

St. Francis heard, it were to him
An emblem of the Seraphim ;
The upward motion of the fire,
The light, the heat, the heart's desire.

Around Assisi's convent gate
The birds, God's poor who cannot wait,
From moor and mire and darksome wood
Came flocking for their dole of food.

" O brother birds," St. Francis said,
" Ye come to me and ask for bread,
But not with bread alone to-day
Shall ye be fed and sent away.

" Ye shall be fed, ye happy birds,
With manna of celestial words ;
Not mine, though mine they seem to be,
Not mine, though they be spoken through me.

" O doubly are ye bound to praise
The great Creator in your lays ;
He giveth you your plumes of down,
Your crimson hoods, your cloaks of brown.

57

THE LITTLE BROWN COMPANY

" He giveth you your wings to fly
And breathe a purer air on high,
And careth for you everywhere,
Who for yourselves do little care ! "

With flutter of swift wings and songs
Together rose the feathered throngs,
And singing scattered far apart ;
Deep peace was in St. Francis' heart.

He knew not if the brotherhood
His homily had understood ;
He only knew that to one ear
The meaning of his words was clear.

HENRY WADSWORTH LONGFELLOW

33

How the Blood flowed afresh from the Effigy of Saint Francis

BEHOLD, in a certain Convent of the Friars Preachers an effigy of Saint Francis with the Holy Stigmata was painted upon the Refectory wall.

A certain Friar of the said Order, beguiled by the doubts begotten of pride in his heart, neither could nor would understand how it had come to pass that Saint Francis had received the most Holy Stigmata. Wherefore, one day, when all the Brethren had withdrawn after their repast, this Friar strode up to the figure, hastily took away the Stigmata, spoiling it, and went his way. Returning thither again upon the same day, Lo ! he saw this effigy adorned with the Holy Stigmata more excellently than heretofore ; whereupon once more he defaced them with malice prepense, and coming back again, he found the painting was repaired. Whereat, in his anger, this Friar damaged the figure once more, in such wise that the wall, wherein it had been limned, was bared entirely. And straightway from that wall, the blood gushed forth violently in exceeding abundance, even as the wine floweth from a full cask when the spigot is drawn ; and splashed the face, the breast and the robe of the Friar, who fell terror-stricken to the ground, lifting up his voice and calling loudly for the Brethren. The entire community was aroused by his cries and hurried to the spot. Astounded and awestruck at the mighty prodigy they hastily collected the blood upon the ground most reverently with a sponge, and caused the said effigy to be repaired in most honourable fashion.

And the elders commanded them that for the credit of the Rule, naught should they reveal thereof to anyone outside the Order. Thereupon quoth that Friar : " Rather will I be cast out from the brotherhood, than conceal the wondrous marvel that honoureth Messer Saint Francis." Yet what requital did the lowly-minded Francis exact from this Friar ? Naught else than that forthwith he made a new man of him ; and in the fervour of his cell he renounced all his books, and waxed great hereafter in prayer. And awhile afterwards, drawing strength from the bosom of Saint Francis, he set forth upon a journey to his church of Ascesi, where in the presence of a number of the Friars' Minor gathered together, humbling himself exceedingly and weeping many tears, he proclaimed the aforesaid miracle, shewing them the blood that he had collected from the ground in the sponge.

A particle whereof he left with them in testimony of the prodigy, and he kept the remainder in blessed memory of Saint Francis. To the praise of Christ. Amen.

Ensamples and Miracles
(Version of M. MANSFIELD, *The Garden Enclosed*)

34
Dun Scotus's Oxford

TOWERY city and branchy between towers ;
    Cuckoo-echoing, bee swarmèd, lark-charmèd, rook-
       racked, river rounded,
The dapple-eared lily below thee ; that country and town
       did
    Once encounter in, here coped and poisèd powers ;

Thou hast a base and brickish skirt there, sours
    That neighbour-nature thy grey beauty is grounded
Best in, graceless growth, thou hast confounded
    Rural rural-keeping folks, flocks, and flowers.

Yet ah ! this air I gather and I release
    He lived on ; these weeds and waters, these wells
       are what
He haunted who of all men sways my spirit to peace.

A reality the rarest veinèd unraveller ; a not
    Rivalled insight be rival Italy or Greece ;
Who fired Thomas for Mary without spot.

GERARD MANLY HOPKINS

35
Franciscan Gossip

JUST before the Feast of All Saints and before Brother
Angellus had come up to London, Brother Richard
of Ingworth and Brother Richard of Devon went on to
Oxford, and there in like manner were received as
Brethren by the Friar Preachers. They ate in their
refectory and slept in their dormitory for eight days, as
though they belonged to the Convent. Afterwards they
obtained a house in the Parish of St. Ebbs, and there they
dwelt without a Chapel until the following summer.
There the sweet Jesus sowed the grains of mustard seed
which was afterwards to become greatest among herbs.

.   .   .   .   .

And sometimes at the evening conference they would
put on the fire a small pot in which were the dregs of beer,
they would dip a cup into the pot and drink in turn, each
speaking meanwhile some word of edification. In like
manner at Salisbury it frequently happened that the
brethren had but the dregs of beer to drink, which they
drank with much merriment and joy at the hour of
conference round the kitchen fire, and he esteemed himself fortunate who could in a friendly way seize the cup
from another.

.   .   .   .   .   .

Brother William related how he once stayed for a long
while at our Convent in Rome, and the Brethren there
had nothing to eat but chestnuts, yet he became so fat
that he was ashamed of himself. He further told me how,
when a youth in his father's house, many beggars came

there to beg, and he would give them his own bread and then beg of them a crust in return, for it seemed to him that a hard crust received in alms for the love of God was sweeter than the delicate food he and his companions were accustomed to eat. Wherefore, that they might thus sweeten their bread, he and other little boys would go and beg from each other in the name of God.

The Lord Abbot of Chertsey also related to me how that a certain friend of the Order of Preachers came to him begging for wood and the Abbot gave him one piece : but his friend said it seemed hard to have been put to so much trouble for the sake of getting but one piece of wood. So the Abbot gave him a second piece of wood. But the Preacher went on to say that as God was a Trinity he ought to have given three pieces ; wherefore the Abbot replied, " By God who is One, thou shalt now have but one piece."

Brother Albert was wont to say that there were three things which glorified the Order, to wit, bare feet, coarse garments, and contempt of money.

THOMAS OF ECCLESTON'S *Chronicle*

(From the version by FATHER CUTHBERT, O.S.F.C.)

63

36

A Franciscan Dream

SWEET and clean and dainty,
  So may she come to me—
Dainty and sweet, on her naked feet,
The Lady Poverty.

A three-roomed cot and a garden plot
For the beasts and the birds and me,
I ask of her, clean and dainty,
The Lady Poverty.

A mug and a bowl and a platter,
And a cup for the passing guest,
A board of deal for the evening meal
At a casement looking west
(At the sunlit goal of the Quest).
A starlit room for slumber
When I flee to the land of Nod—
No curtain drawn to hide the dawn.
And a window giving on God.
(Far o'er the hills untrod).

Christ on His Cross above me,
To make the white walls fair ;
Our Lady's face to gain me grace,
And an image of sweet St. Clare.

Dainty and meek and holy,
So shall she come to me,
In russet gown, with her eyes cast down,
The Lady Poverty.

64

THE LITTLE BROWN COMPANY

And a guest room for the Christ Child
When all the inns are shut—
To rest His limb, and shelter Him,
A hut beside my hut.
Loving and kind and tender,
So shall she come to me
With food for two the whole year through
The Lady Poverty.

Teapot brew and porridge,
And whatever the good God sends,
A log ablaze on winter days
For me and my four-foot friend
(And whomever the good God send).

Books on a shelf beside me
To lift my soul from earth—
A book of prayer and a book of praise,
And a little book of mirth.

Flowers to deck my garden,
These shall my Lady bring,
Strewing her rosy riches,
And her lilies clad like a king,
And a cabbage patch shall she vote me,
And a spade to turn the clod,
And Francis bless my handiness
With a dream of the Garden of God.
With a tool and a book and a platter,
So be my Lady sent ;
So shall she scheme with a task and a dream,
The joy of a full content,
Tender and sweet and dainty,
So may she come to me,
In humble guise, with her starry eyes,
The Lady Poverty.

ENID DINNIS

E   65

37

In Praise of Poverty

THEY were no fools, those old saints, in their appraisement of the good things of life. Rather are we foolish in labelling as good the things which they forswore. It *is* the immaterial things which are material ; the material do not matter in the least. But what we hold as a more or less fanciful ideal they held practically and found in their tenure a joy, a gaiety which our more discreet sophistry is powerless to attain. It is, indeed, part of the divine reasonableness that the things which are foolishness with God do not make for even earthly happiness. He in whose sight a thousand years are as one day may conceivably have forseen a world's development. At any rate there have been some content to take Him at His word, nor are men lacking that have called them mad ; yet their true title was evolved of universal judgment and that title is . . . " The Saints of God." Out of our own mouths we stand condemned. We canonize those few who practised what we, by our lives, profess to disbelieve. And, really, the Saints chose not merely the better but the easier part. Theirs is a rule of life how circumspect and yet how simple. To take God's words as they stand saves an infinity of trouble, and if they do not hold water the responsibility is His, not ours. Does such a principle seem crude, unenterprizing ? Then is there comfort for some of us, as for them, in that old stipulation concerning the Kingdom and a little child.

Ah, Lady Poverty, but after all has disputation any place in your affairs ?

THE LITTLE BROWN COMPANY

" She dwelleth in the Holy Mountains. The giants have not been able to reach unto the print-marks of her feet and eagles have not soared so high as unto her neck. Yet because she is liberal of heart is she easily seen of those who love and found of those who seek her."

And thus, bringing her case to court, it is borne in upon me that I, who had not the wit to want her and found her only unawares, make but a sorry advocate. Nevertheless, one argument I have, for me predominant ; an argument to be ignored, perhaps, but not confuted ; the argument of Francis and his brethren.

" *At His birth faithfully didst thou come to meet Him . . . nor didst thou leave Him in the hour of His death.*" Surely, *this* is her plea of pleas. Whilst all else on earth forsook the Son of God, Poverty was faithful, so that nothing in Him appeared more glorious than herself. It has been, in truth, a strange perversion that makes despicable her whose company the Lord of Heaven kept. The stable—the carpenter's shop—the three years' vagabondage—the Passion's ignominy—how uncompromising is their uniformity. I have wondered sometimes whether, walking the world in purple and fine linen, we shall not be ashamed at long last, to look Him in the face. I have wondered whether an honest love of Him does not demand, as those old Saints insisted, a love also of the way He chose ; whether, indeed, by paths too alien we can be His followers at all.

MADELEINE NIGHTINGALE
(From *The Confessions of a Cottager*)

38

The Singing Saint

HE sung of earth—so fair a lay,
   That Heaven stole his song away,
And rapt he stood to serenade
The Lady Poverty, God's maid.
His praise a spangled web did spin
To snare the whole creation in,
And all wild things of field and wood
He called into his brotherhood.
He sang of Life immortal slain,
In songs that strove with tears of pain,
Till, arrow-like from earthly sod,
His singing pierced the Heart of God,
And swift returning answer came
In living tongues of wounding flame,
That made in hands and feet and side
New mouths to sing Christ crucified.

.   .   .   .   .   .

The lips of years in leisured line
Have worn the stone about his shrine,
But still the Pentecostal breeze,
That ceaseless sings in Sion's trees,
Is murmurous with his melody ;
And in her heart Humanity
Stores for a balm to heal and bless,
The fragrance of his mirthfulness.

SISTER MARY BENEVENTUA, O.P.
(Dorothy I. Little)

39
Knights of the Round Table
(THE WHITSUNTIDE CHAPTER)

FROM all the places and hermitages of the Order brethren came, many of them newly received novices who had not yet looked upon the face of Francis.

They came from Lombardy and Apulia, from Terra di Lavoro and the mountains overlooking the Adriatic, in fact from every Italian province. For many of them it was a home-coming ; they knew the Porziuncula and loved the shade of its surrounding wood where they had prayed and felt the stirrings of the heavenly life which nowhere seemed so near and so real as in the silences of that holy place. And to the novices and those who had not yet been there, it was the turning of their faces towards the Holy Zion from the captivity in which they had been born. The glory of their vocation was still altogether gathered up in Francis and the wattle huts near Assisi.

As the brethren met and welcomed each other their tongues betrayed their origin or upbringing. Some spoke with their native grace of noble birth ; others with the acquired distinction of the schools ; whilst others had only the art of speech which they had learned toiling for daily bread. The soft sibilant utterance of Umbria mingled with the guttural dialects of Lombardy and the strident tones of the South. But here and there was a brother whose words bespoke a corner from beyond the Alps ; one who passing through Italy had met the brethren and joined their ranks . . .

Not the least uplifted in spirit was Francis as he gazed upon these elect companions. To him it was a renewal of the joy of adventure he had felt in the first days of his own missionary journeys. Nor could he long resist the call their hardihood made to him. Taking aside some of the brethren he addressed them : My best beloved, it is but right that I should be a pattern and example to all the brethren. I have sent brethren into far-off parts to undergo much labour and shame and hunger and thirst and other necessities ; it is only just therefore, and holy obedience requires, that I too go forth into some distant land ; and so will the brethren be encouraged to endure patiently their adversities when they hear that I suffer the same. Go therefore and pray that the Lord may grant me to make choice of the province that shall be most to His praise and the profit of souls and the encouragement of the brethren.

Father Cuthbert, O.S.F.C.
Life of St. Francis

40

The Little Black Hen

WE hear the little hen was black,
    And nothing hen-wise did she lack—
Besides her pow'r of laying eggs,
This hen had feathers down her legs.

Just like a tame dove's were her feet,
('Twas unexpected this, but sweet),
And oh ! her chicks so many were,
She couldn't keep them under her.

.   .   .   .   .

One of the very best of men
Once dreamed about this little hen :
And when the sleeping Saint awoke,
He pondered long before he spoke.

" I am that hen, in stature small,
So black by nature that I crawl
Instead of, like the simple dove,
Seeking the sky with wings of love.

" I am not able to defend
My chicks and those the Lord will send.
Take, Holy Church, my offerings
Beneath the shadow of thy wings.

.   .   .   .   .

THE LITTLE BROWN COMPANY

When later on, he saw the Pope,
He told him of his ardent hope . . .
Honorius blessed the little hen
Who wasn't black—whose chicks were men.

ARMEL O'CONNOR
The Poor Man of Assisi

41
St. Anthony of Padua

TO Assisi, then, went Antony—twenty-six years of age—and witnessed there the wonders of generosity that fed three thousand friars, and saw for the first time the gentle figure of Francis. The Chapter was presided over by Elias of Corlona—the Vicar General—and Francis just sat quietly at his feet, only intervening once at the last session when he was seen to draw his Vicar's attention by pulling his habit, and then to whisper something to him. Evidently it was about the proposed renewal of the mission to Germany, and Elias made an immediate appeal for volunteers. Ninety came forward at once, but not Antony. Standing there lonely, silent, unknown amidst three thousand brothers, he was in no mood to wander further into strange lands ; something else was in his mind. The Chapter was dispersing, the Provincial ministers were fixing the final assignations for their subjects, if he did not hurry he would be left at the disposition of the Vicar General. So Antony went up to Brother Gratian, Minister of the Province of Romagna (then including all Lombardy), and begged him to take him in his company. Not a word about his qualifications, his studies, his past, just—it seems possible—a mention of his priesthood.

Brother Gratian, true to his name, welcomed the lonely friar : he went north with him, and willingly then allowed him to retire to a little hermitage of his Province at Monte Paolo, near Forli. Here Antony, true to the traditions of the Order, prepared himself in austerity and solitude for the work of preaching, destined for him by

God. Severe indeed was his life during these next few months.

Not, perhaps, every day, but on Sunday, doubtless, and holidays Antony would say mass for the little Community. He always assisted at matins and then would retire to a little cell apart, spend his day in solitude and prayer ; though making a point of always rejoining his brethren at the hour of dinner. So weak did he become that he had to be supported to and from his little cell to the convent. How far have we travelled from the Canon of Holy Cross, the student, the Guest-master ; how far, too, from the ardent young friar bent on martyrdom. Antony was learning, quicker even than his father, Francis, the secret of religious service—self-surrender before God's will.

DOMINIC DEVAS, O.F.M.
Franciscan Essays

42

Appreciation à la Mode

A LADY in the latest gown
    Speaks to me thus in London Town :
" Of all the Saints that really were,
I almost think that I prefer
Francesco of Assisi.   He
Seems absolutely *sweet* to me."
Then to her looking-glass she goes
And puts fresh powder on her nose.

Many a mile from London Town
A happy spirit, clad in brown,
Ragged but woodland-scented, clean,
Dances and sings before his Queen.
Phantom but ringing laughter fills
Wide heavens over noble hills,
When Fashion deigns to call him *sweet*,
Who bled from heart and hands and feet.

ARMEL O'CONNOR
The Poor Man of Assisi

43

The Begging Friar

LAST summer in Rome I lodged at the Hotel de Russié, and in the archway of the courtyard of that mansion, waited usually, in the mornings, a Capuchin friar, begging for his monastery. Now, though I greatly object to any clergyman's coming and taking me by the throat, and saying, " Pay me that thou owest," I never pass a begging friar without giving him sixpence, or the equivalent fivepence of foreign coin ; extending the charity even occasionally as far as tenpence, if no five-penny bit chances to be in my purse. And this particular begging friar having a gentle face, and a long white beard, and a beautiful cloak, like a blanket ; and being altogether the pleasantest sight, next to Sandro Botticelli's Zipporah, I was like to see in Rome in the course of the day, I always gave him the extra fivepence for looking so nice ; which generosity so worked on his mind,—(the more usual English religious sentiment in Rome expending itself rather in buying poetical pictures of monks than in filling their bellies)—that, after some six or seven doles of tenpence he must needs take my hand one day, and try to kiss it. Which being only just able to prevent, I took him round the neck and kissed his lips instead ; and this, it seems, was more to him than the tenpences, for, next day, he brought me a little reliquary, with a certified fibre in it of St. Francis' cloak (the hair one, now preserved at Assisi) ; and when afterwards I showed my friend Fra Antonio, the Assisi sacristan, what I had got, it was a pleasure to see him open his eyes, wider than Monsieur the Syndic at Hansli's fifty-thousand crowns. He thought

76

THE LITTLE BROWN COMPANY

I must have come by it dishonestly ; but not I, a whit, for I most carefully explained to the Capuchin, when he brought it to me, that I was more a Turk than a Catholic ; but he said I might keep the reliquary, for all that.

JOHN RUSKIN
Fors Clavigera, Letter LVI

44

Ode on the Visit of St. Francis to the Holy Land

(This ode was written at the request of the Custos of the Holy
Land on the occasion of the Seventh Centenary celebrations in
honour of St. Francis' visit to the Holy Land, held at Jerusalem,
October 1919.)

IN thee, fair land, the holiest of our race
   Their wonders wrought and prophesied and prayed.
To saint and seer thou gavest resting place,
Thy winds caressed them and thy trees gave shade.
Thou art the wonderland of our dull earth,
Thou art the treasure-place of heavenly lore.
In thee, as in an earthly paradise,
The sinless maid had birth
Who 'mid thy snows the Babe of Heaven bore,
The Babe of love and woe and sacrifice.

And for all time His presence made thee holy,
The Blessed One who dwelt in thee of old :
The King at whose Divine touch things most lowly
Were made more precious far than kingly gold.
O land of ever blessed memory where
He prayed and suffered for a fallen race !
Land of the holy wars.   Have I but dreamed,
Or saw I banners fair
On which was pictured many a holy face,
And lances that like lights on altars gleamed ?

I lived a brief space in a bygone day,
I looked into the past and saw a throng
Of pagan foes and then the vast array
Of Christian knights, high-crested, proud and strong.

78

THE LITTLE BROWN COMPANY

And there I saw a man of humble mien,
Who bore not sword nor mail nor did aspire
To knightly fame and yet a soul had he
For noble deeds most keen,
For Thou, Lord, gavest him a twofold desire—
To raise dead souls to life and die for Thee.

Most faithful knight with warfare weak and pale,
Warfare with viewless foes on unseen field.
He strove not like Thy knights in helm and mail
Whose weapons were the simple sword and shield.
Who were indeed on high adventure bound,
Whose spirits were by noble purpose swayed,
Who in rude conflict put Thy foes to flight,
Striving for holy ground,
But subtle foes against man's soul arrayed
Did Francis meet and vanquish day and night.

A rich reward he sought and not in vain,
This fair-souled knight of Christ-like chivalry ;
This dweller in the desert place of pain
Which was a paradise because of Thee.
He sought the palm which is the martyr's prize.
Wish most sublime fulfilled in later years.
Thou gavest him martyr's wounds with Thine own
      hand,
This knight of paradise,
Now Thy companion in Thy saintly spheres,
One of Thy chosen in *Thy Holy Land.*

                    FATHER ADRIAN, O.F.M.

79

45

Commemoration

THERE is not a more religious building on earth than the Church of St. Francis at Assisi. To enter it, as I once did, at sunset on the eve of St. Francis' Day, the moment at which he passed, to see the Giotto frescoes of the roof lit by the rays of the setting sun, to find the Bishop of Assisi surrounded by his brothers and by the townsfolk singing the First Vespers of the Feast, is to pass into a scene and atmosphere of heavenly beauty. Better still is to kneel at the tomb on the morning of the day itself while the peasantry come very early for their communions, crowding round the priest as he stands at the tomb, and being fed by him as he divides many Hosts and places their fragments in the open mouths of Francis' children, who have come to be fed with the Bread of Life, after the manner of Francis' birds.

REV. H. F. B. MACKAY
The Message of Francis of Assisi

46
The Irish Franciscan

A BAREFOOT friar all in brown,
Weather-beat face and storm-rent gown,
Tattered hood over shaven crown,
Travelled as the sun goes down.

Whither ere morning goeth he
Over the bog he moveth free ;
Bog so brown it were hard to see
That brown man travelling patiently.

Hidden under his threadbare best
He holdeth One close to his breast :
" O Lord, in what poor place of rest
This winter's eve thou harbourest ! "

Deep in the pools the red lights die,
Darkness veileth the western sky ;
Only the plovers cry and cry
Amen to prayers as they flitter by.

Who are these, thou barefoot man,
Weak and weary and under a ban,
Who meet thee in the starlight wan ?
Columb, and Patrick and Adamnan !

Three with torches faint and white,
Threading the holes to give thee light,
Bowing before the One of might
Thou barest with thee through the night.

THE LITTLE BROWN COMPANY

Now the dawn opens in the east,
There's the altar, and here the priest ;
Welcome now to the last and least,
Who hunger for the Master's feast.

Table of rock, and cloth of moss ;
(Gold and silver are Mammon's dross),
Rude is the stone, and rude the cross,
O Christ our gain, O World our loss !

Ye banned and outlawed of the faith !
Shrive ye now with bated breath ;
Hither the hunter hasteneth,
Fear not the little pain of death.

Shines the moon on the curling sea,
Sighs the wind in the white-thorn tree ;
Forth from the bough as the gale blows free
Swingeth a figure dolorously.

A barefoot friar all in brown,
Weather-beat face and threadbare gown,
Girdle of rope and shaven crown—
Swingeth he as the moon goes down.

Rosa Mulholland
(Lady Gilbert)

47

Christmas at Greccio

SINCE his trip to the Holy Land and his visit to Bethlehem, St. Francis had a special devotion to the Christmas time. One year the festival fell on a Friday, and Brother Morico propounded to the brethren the opinion that for that reason meat might not be eaten on Christmas day. " If it is Christmas it is not Friday," replied Francis. " If the walls could eat flesh, I would give them it to-day, but as they cannot, I will at least rub them over with it ! " He often said of this day: " If I knew the Emperor, I would ask him that all would be ordered on this day to throw out corn to the birds, especially to our sisters the larks, and that everyone who has a beast in the stable should give them a specially good feed for the love of the Child Jesus born in a manger. And this day the rich should feast the poor."

In the year 1223 Francis himself celebrated Christmas in a way the world had never seen the match of. In Greccio he had a friend and well-wisher, Messer John Vellita, who had given him and his brothers a wood-grown cliff up above Greccio, for them to live there. Francis now had the man called to Colombo and said to him : " I want to celebrate the holy Christmas night along with thee, and now listen, how I have thought it out for myself. In the woods by the cloister thou will find a cave and there thou mayst arrange a manger filled with hay. There must also be an ox and an ass, just as in Bethlehem. I want for men to celebrate seriously the coming of the Son of God upon earth and see with my own eyes how poor and miserable He wished to be for our sakes."

John Vellita looked after all of Francis' wishes, and at midnight of Christmas eve the Brothers came together to celebrate the festival of Christmas. All carried lighted torches, and around the manger the Brothers stood with their candles, so that it was as light as the day under the dark vaulting of the rock. Mass was read over the manger as the altar, so that the Divine Child under the forms of bread and wine should Himself come to the place, as bodily and discernibly He had been in the stable of Bethlehem. For a moment it seemed to John Vellita that he saw a real child lying in the manger, but as if dead or sleeping. Then Brother Francis stepped forward and took it lovingly in his arms, and the child smiled at Francis, and with his little hands stroked his bearded chin and his coarse grey habit. And yet this vision did not astonish Messer Giovanni (John). For Jesus had been dead or else asleep in many hearts, but Brother Francis had by his voice and by his example again restored the Divine Child to life.

JOHANNES JÖRGENSEN, *Life of St. Francis*
(T. O'CONNOR SLOANE'S translation)

48

The Stigmata of St. Francis

NATURE to him displayed her loveliness,
   The beauty of the bird and flower and tree.
He spake with all a poet's tenderness,
With saintly gratitude and courtesy :
" All days, O fairest earth, to my poor breast
Thy gracious beauty a delight will be,
Yet in thy love I have not final rest,
Yet for a fairer loveliness I pine.
Thy beauty—like the rose flush of the east
That of the rising splendour gives a sign—
Bids me remember that which I pursue,
The vision of a glory all divine
Which yet may break (hope whispers) on my view,
The vision of the beautiful and true."

Such was thy guest, and even on this earth
On heavenly beauty 'twas thy joy to gaze,
The sunrise of thy hope from Heaven shone forth
And pierced thee with its vivifying rays.
And in Christ's garden like a passion flower
Didst thou become.   Men saw thee with amaze,
For thou, like Christ, wast wounded in that hour,
O Francis, on thy hands and feet and side ;
But not by human or by fiendish power,
Thy wounds came not from envy, hate and pride.
Thou wast the victim of no cruel foe,
Like those against thy Master once allied.
Men wounded Him their bitter hate to show,
He wounded thee because He loved thee so.

FATHER ADRIAN, O.F.M.

85

49

Feast of the Stigmata at Mount La Verna

WE rose at midnight for Matins. The weather had changed. A mountain storm was raging in full fury. The rain poured in torrents, the wind howled, distant thunder rumbled angrily. What a spectacle the church presented ! On the benches, in the Confessionals, underneath the altars, on the Altar steps, lay the recumbent figures of a hundred or two peasants who had found no other place to rest their heads. Great green Ginghams were stretched out to dry ; dogs slept by their master's side, nearly every man had his bundles of provisions.

Verily these Tuscan peasants are at home in their Father's house. As the Matin's bell rang out, the dripping creatures rose and shook themselves, and soon the rattle of Rosaries showed that they too were joining in the Divine Praises. Matins and Lauds were chanted to the Tones (not monotoned) in honour of the great Feast. And then followed that wonderful procession along the *loggia* to the Chapel of the Stigmata. Crucifer with his Crucifix, on either side of him two acolytes with octagonal lanterns raised aloft on staves, led the way of the long procession of St. Francis' sons chanting the *Miserere*, and we followed with the medley group of motley peasants. In the Chapel itself there was room only for the Friars who knelt in a double row with outstretched arms ; the rest of us remained crowded at the open door. And presently on the very spot where the Poor Man of Assisi was transformed into the likeness of his Crucified Master, the rich clear voice of the

Versicularian intoned the versicle, *Signati Domine servum tuum Franciscum :—Signis Redemptionis Nostrae !* came the answering shout from hundreds of throats, some of them choked by the tears which it was so difficult to keep back.

It was half-past two in the morning ere the long religious function was over. Many of the Fathers did not go back to bed, but betook themselves straight to their Confessionals. The long series of Masses began about three o'clock. That day some two thousand confessions were heard, some two thousand souls received Holy Communion. Communion was still being given after midday to people who had been waiting hours for a chance of going to Confession, and they were fasting be it remembered. Many had to go away with their devotion unsatisfied.

The Fathers fed, entirely, about a thousand people, and partially, quite double that number. And all this—all this—because the son of an Umbrian cloth merchant, nearly seven hundred years ago, chose the bitter part and loved God above all things, and his neighbour better than himself.

MONTGOMERY CARMICHAEL
In Tuscany

50

Democracies

I SEE the world's democracies,
    Upheld by myriad spears,
Watching with greedy hatred
Each other through the years.

But, Oh ! to see democracies,
No gold lust might divide,
With armaments the slender lance
That pierced the Godhead's side.

W. E. Awde

THE LITTLE BROWN COMPANY

51

The Social Teaching of St. Francis

POVERTY had set the brethren free from the world
of barter and gain, of avarice and usury and of the
hatreds that rose therefrom.   It was, moreover, as he saw
it a sort of charter of possession in the things of the earth ;
it gave a man a lien upon and in some way bound him up
with the material world.   The man who has money holds
the earth in bondage ; his money thrusts him between God
and God's creatures, and too often he prostitutes the earth
which is God's to his own selfish pleasure, and that to
Francis was an unholy thing.   " The Earth is the Lord's,"
expresses in a very intimate phrase, the faith of Francis
concerning the use men should make of this visible
creation ; and whatever tended to blur that faith he
abhorred with all the passionate sincerity of his nature.
It was not that he had any theories against the right of
private property : in fact he accepted that right so far as
it concerned others who were not of his fraternity : that
was their concern and the concern of the Church.   But he
grieved over the abuse of the right, and in his dealing with
men of the world who sought his counsel he always
insisted that their property was a trust put into their
hands by the providence of God, not for their own benefit
alone, but for the benefit of all who were in need.   But
for himself and the brethren he held that God had set them
free from this trust in order that they might more con-
vincingly by word and example warn the world against
the dangers and lust of wealth.   The very existence of
the brotherhood dependent upon the goodwill of men
for their bodily sustenance, would be a continual reproach

to the avaricious, and an invitation to those who held this world's goods, to fulfil their trust in relieving the needs of the poor.   Hence in sending the brethren out to beg, he would say to them : " Go forth ; for in this last hour the Friars' Minor have been placed in the world that the elect may fulfil those things for which the Great Judge will commend them saying : ' What you did to these My lesser brethren you did unto Me.' "

FATHER CUTHBERT, O.S.F.C.
Life of St. Francis of Assisi

52

At Assisi

(Giotto's *Sancta Paupertas*)

HER head, whereon the veil was wound,
    By her own hair is meetly bound,
With roses red and white around,
And lilies on a golden ground.
(I heard her call to me).
And though her feet with thorns are shod,
No way more sweetly turns to God,
Than doth the way she sweetly trod,
The Lady Poverty.

I linger where her feet have led,
I see the paths whereon they bled,
I think of him whom once she wed
Who died her spouse and lives being dead,
And still she calls to me ;
For in her converse is content,
Nor all the years that came and went
Could rob of her blest blandishment
The Lady Poverty.

Her face is gentler than the skies,
But in the depth of her meek eyes
Dwells wonder and a mild surprise
That fools mistake her lovely guise.
(Surely she calls to me).
And wisdom doth my heart decoy.
And all my pride it doth destroy,

91

THE LITTLE BROWN COMPANY

For in thy voice there liveth joy,
My Lady Poverty.

I know not whence that joy was born,
I know men hold that joy in scorn ;
'Tis they, not thou, who walk forlorn,
Thou dost the crown of Christ adorn
And keep His company ;
So, having naught, possessing all,
Thou dost the whole world hold in thrall,
Me thy most lowly slave install,
O Lady Poverty.

MADELEINE NIGHTINGALE
Verses Wise and Otherwise

53
Franciscan Art

YOU are in the chapel next the high altar of the great Franciscan church of Florence. A few hundred yards west of it, within ten minutes' walk, is the Baptistry of Florence . . . Now, that little octagon Baptistry stood where it now stands (and was finished though the roof has been altered since) in the eighth century. It is the central building of Etrurian Christianity,—of European Christianity.

From the day it was finished Christianity went on doing her best, in Etruria and elsewhere, for four hundred years, and her best seemed to have come to very little,—when there rose up two men who vowed to God it should come to more, and they made it come to more forthwith. The two men were the two great religious Powers and Re- formers of the thirteenth century ; St. Francis who taught Christian men how they should behave, and St. Dominic who taught Christian men what they should think. In brief, one the Apostle of Works ; the other of Faith. Each sent his little company of disciples to teach and preach in Florence. St. Francis in 1212 ; St. Dominic in 1220. The little companies were settled one ten minutes' walk east of the old Baptistry ; the other five minutes' walk west of it. And after they had stayed quietly in such lodgings as were given them, preaching and teaching through most of the century ; and had got Florence, as it were, heated through, she burst out into Christian poetry and architecture, of which you have heard much talk : burst into bloom Arnolfo, Giotto, Dante, Orcagna and the like persons . . . The Dominicans designed their

93

own buildings ; but for the Franciscans and the town worked the first great master of Gothic art, Arnolfo, with Giotto at his side and Dante looking on, and whispering sometimes a word to both.

And here you stand beside the high altar of the Franciscan church, under a vault of Arnolfo's building, with at least some of Giotto's colour on it still fresh ; and in front of you, over the little altar, is a reportedly authentic portrait of St. Francis, taken from life by Giotto's master. . . .

Cimabrue, Etruscan born, gave, we saw, the life of the Norman to the tradition of the Greek, eager action to holy contemplation.

And what more is left for his favourite shepherd boy Giotto to do, than this, except to paint with ever increasing skill. He evidently never checked the boy from the first day he found him. Showed him all he knew : talked with him of many things he felt himself unable to paint : made him a workman and a gentleman,—above all, a Christian,—yet left him a shepherd. And Heaven had made him such a painter, that at his height, the words of his epitaph are in nowise overwrought : *Ille ego sum, per quem pictura extincta revixit.*

JOHN RUSKIN
Mornings in Florence

54

Paradiso

(From Canto XI)

BETWEEN Tupino and the wave that falls
   From blest Ubaldo's chosen hill, there hangs
Rich slope of mountain high, whence heat and cold
Are wafted through Perugia's eastern gate :
And Nocera with Gualdo, in its rear,
Mourn for their heavy yoke. Upon that side,
Where it doth break its steepness most, arose
A sun upon the world, as duly this
From Ganges doth : therefore let none, who speak
Of that place, say Ascesi ; for its name
Were lamely so deliver'd ; but the East,
To call things rightly, be it henceforth styled.
He was not yet much distant from his rising,
When his good influence 'gan to bless the earth.
A dame, to whom none openeth pleasure's gate
More than to death, was 'gainst his father's will,
His stripling choice : and he did make her his,
Before the spiritual court by nuptial bonds,
And in his father's sight : from day to day,
Then loved her more devoutly. She bereaved
Of her first husband, slighted and obscure,
Thousand and hundred years and more, remain'd
Without a single suitor, till he came.
Nor aught avail'd that, with Amyclas she
Was found unmoved at rumour of his voice,
Who shook the world : nor aught her constant boldness
Whereby with Christ she mounted on the Cross,

95

When Mary stay'd beneath. But not to deal
Thus closely with thee longer, take at large
The lovers' titles—Poverty and Francis.
Their concord and glad looks, wonder and love,
And sweet regard gave birth to holy thoughts,
So much that venerable Bernard first,
Did bare his feet, and, in pursuit of peace
So heavenly, ran, yet deem'd his footing slow.
O hidden riches ! O prolific good !
Egidius bares him next, and next Sylvester,
And follow, both, the bridegroom : so the bride
Can please them.   Thenceforth goes he on his way,
The father and the master, with his spouse,
And with that family, whom now the cord
Girt humbly : nor did abjectness of heart,
Weigh down his eyelids, for that he was son
Of Pietro Bernardone and by men
In wondrous sort despised.   But royally
His hard intention he to Innocent
Set forth ; and from him first received the seal
On his religion.   Then, when numerous flock'd
The tribe of lowly ones, that traced *his* steps,
Whose marvellous life deservedly were sung
In heights empyreal ; through Honorius' hand
A second crown to deck their Guardians' virtues,
Was by the eternal Spirit inwreath'd : and when
He had, through thirst of martyrdom, stood up
In the proud Soldan's presence, and there preach'd
Christ and for his followers, but found the race
Unripen'd for conversion : back once more
He hasted, (not to intermit his toil),
And reaped Ausonian Lands.   On the hard rock,
'Twixt Arno and the Tiber, he from Christ
Took the last signet, which his limbs two years
Did carry.   Then, the season come that he,
Who to such good had destined him, was pleased

THE LITTLE BROWN COMPANY

To advance him to the meed, which he had earn'd
By his self-humbling : to his brotherhood,
As their just heritage, he gave in charge
His dearest lady : and enjoin'd their love
And faith to her : and, from her bosom will'd
His goodly spirit should move forth, returning
To its appointed kingdom : nor would have
His body laid upon another bier.

DANTE
(CARY's Version)

55

The Blessing of Brother Leo

ST. FRANCIS told Brother Leo, whom alone he kept with him, to bring him bread and water once a day towards evening, and leave them at the little door of his shelter. At midnight he was to come and call him for Matins and Lauds, but was not to enter suddenly. He was to stand outside and intone the versicle : *Domine labia mea aperies*, and if the second part of this versicle, " And my mouth will announce Thy praise," were answered from within, he was to go in, but if it was not said he was to go away. The Saint's devout companion observed these directions to the letter, being anxious above all to assist and obey him in all things ; but often he had to go back of a stormy night, for the Saint was frequently in ecstasy and would make no answer. This zealous service of his companion, the Saint repaid by delivering him from a most grievous temptation, not of the flesh, but of the spirit, which he dared not explain to his Spiritual Father, for he was overcome with shame. But while he was longing to obtain some words written out by the Saint with his own hand, by which writing he believed he would escape his affliction, or at least bear it the more easily, the holy Master learning from on high the trouble and the desire of his disciple, ordered a piece of paper and some ink to be brought, and wrote the Blesssing which follows, placing before it a large mysterious Thau, or letter T.

May The Lord bless thee and keep thee.
The Lord show His face to thee and have mercy on thee.
The Lord turn his countenance to thee and give thee
Brother Leo may our Lord bless thee.   [peace.

FATHER PASCHAL ROBINSON's Version

56

A Franciscan Prayer

WHEN I am old and tutored by
   The grim experience of days ;
When I have proved men in their ways,
Oh, do not let the dreamer die.

When I have learned aside to toss
The foolish things that wise men hate,
Lest Littleness should hold me great
Be mine the folly of the Cross.

When comes detachment's strength to me,
Let mine the weakness be that wept
O'er Lazarus's grave and kept
Three comrades in Gethsemane.

When head bids heart herself forget,
When Reason's lure would love deceive,
May my poor foolish heart achieve
A few life-giving blunders yet.

When I have grown too sane, too sad,
To join the angels' faerie ring
And serve the play-time of the King,
Then, sweet St. Francis, make me mad.

                    ENID DINNIS

57
The Sacristan's Cell

I AM now sitting in the Sacristan's cell at Assisi. Its roof is supported by three massive beams—not squared beams, but tree trunks barked, with the grand knots left in them, answering all the purpose of sculpture. The walls are rude white plaster, though there is a Crucifixion by Giottino on the back of one, outside the door ; the floor, brick ; the table, olive wood ; the windows two, and only about four feet by two in the opening (but giving plenty of light in the sunny morning aided by the white walls), looking out on the valley of the Tescio. Under one of them, a small arched stove for cooking ; in a square niche beside the other, an iron wash-hand stand,—that is to say, a tripod of good fourteenth century work, carrying a grand brown porringer, two feet across, and half a foot deep. Between the windows is the fireplace, the wall above it rich brown with the smoke. Hung against the wall behind me are a saucepan, gridiron, and toasting fork ; and in the wall a little door, closed only by a brown canvas curtain, opening to an inner cell nearly filled by the bedstead ; and at the side of the room a dresser, with cupboard below, and two wine flasks, and three pots of Raphael were on the top of it, together with the first volume of the *Maraviglie di Dio nell' anime del Purgatorio, del padre Carlo Gregorio Rossignoli, della Compagnia di Gesu (Roma,* 1841). There is a bird singing outside, a constant low hum of flies, making the ear sure it is summer ; a dove cooing, very low ; and absolutely nothing else to be heard, I find, after listening with great care. And I feel entirely at home, because the room—except in the one point of being extremely dirty—is just the kind of thing I used to see in my aunt's bakehouse ; and the country and the sweet valley outside still rest in peace, such as used to be on the Surrey hills in the olden days.

JOHN RUSKIN
(*Fors Clavigera*, Letter XLVI.,
28th Aug., 1874)

58

Canticle of the Sun

MOST high, omnipotent, good Lord,
  Praise, glory and honour and benediction, all are
    Thine.
To Thee alone do they belong, most High,
And there is no man fit to mention Thee.

Praise be to Thee, my Lord, with all Thy creatures,
Especially to my worshipful brother sun,
The which lights up the day, and through him dost Thou
    brightness give ;
And beautiful is he and radiant with splendour great ;
Of Thee, most High, signification gives.

Praised be my Lord, for sister moon and for the stars,
In heaven Thou hast formed them clear and precious
    and fair.

Praised be my Lord for brother wind
And for the air and clouds and fair and every kind of
    weather,
By the which Thou givest to Thy creatures nourishment,

Praised be My Lord for sister water,
The which is greatly helpful and humble and precious
    and pure.

Praised be my Lord for brother fire,
By the which Thou lightest up the dark.
And fair is he and gay and mighty and strong.

THE LITTLE BROWN COMPANY

Praised be my Lord for our sister, mother earth,
The which sustains and keeps us
And brings forth diverse fruits with grass and flowers
    bright.

Praised be my Lord for those who for Thy love forgive
And weakness bear and tribulation.
Blessed those who shall in peace endure,
For by Thee, most High, shall they be crowned.

Praised be my Lord for our sister, the bodily death,
From the which no living man can flee.
Woe to them who die in mortal sin ;
Blessed those who shall find themselves in Thy most holy
    will,
For the second death shall do them no ill,
Praise ye and bless ye my Lord, and give Him thanks,
And be subject unto Him with great humility.

Translation by
FATHER PASCHAL ROBINSON, O.F.M.

59

Deus Meus Et Omnia

I AM not privileged to climb and tread
   The heights and steeps that holy Francis trod ;
I am not worthy, O my Lord and God,
To meet Thee in communion so dread—
Wide as a cross, my eager arms to spread,
And taste within my very bones and blood,
The quintessential anguish of the rood,
And see this flesh with Thine own wounds made red.

Yet at Alverna's altar let me fall,
There to adore while my most valiant priest
Meets that embrace so fearful and so fair ;
Then with the golden splendour of the East,
Then with the tuneful sisters of the air,
Loud let me praise Thee, " O my God, my All ! "

R. E.

60

The Example of Brother Leo, when St. Francis commanded him to wash the stone

AS St. Francis was speaking with Brother Leo one day
on Mount Alvernia he said to him :

" Brother Little Sheep, wash this stone with water."
And forthwith Brother Leo fetched water and washed it.
With great joy and delight St. Francis said :

" Wash it with wine " ; and he did so.

" Wash it," said St. Francis again, " with oil " ; and
this also was done.   Then said St. Francis :

" Brother Little Sheep, wash this stone with balsam,"
and Brother Leo replied : " O sweet Father, how should
I have balsam in so wild a place as this ? "   And St.
Francis said to him : " Know, Brother Little Sheep of
Christ, that this is the stone on which Christ sat when
once He appeared to me here : and therefore I bade thee
wash it four times without answering me, because Jesus
Christ promised me four singular graces for my Order.
The first is, that all who love my Order and the Brothers
sincerely, shall have the grace of final perseverance, and
by the divine favour make a good end.   The second, that
all who persecute this Order shall be notably punished.
The third is that no wicked man, persevering in his
wickedness, shall be able to remain long in the Order.
The fourth, that this Order shall continue to the
Judgment Day."

The Fioretta

61

Mount Alvernia

A DARK blue crest in the azure skies,
⠀⠀The long, brown slopes below—
Unto the hill lift up thine eyes,
⠀⠀Lift up thy heart also.
Dark-crown'd, outstanding
⠀⠀Aloof, commanding
⠀⠀⠀⠀La Verna.

Over the world it stands enthroned,
⠀⠀It stands, Heaven's own watch-tower,
Over the world and its ways disowned,
⠀⠀Over the clamant hour.
A stronghold stark,
⠀⠀A refuge-ark,
⠀⠀⠀⠀La Verna.

Legate of Heaven and interceder,
⠀⠀Lover of souls and friend,
Giver of grace to every needer,
⠀⠀Chanting the chant without end,
A treasure city,
⠀⠀Of love and pity,
⠀⠀⠀⠀La Verna.

Crown'd with many a cross, and chiming
⠀⠀With benison of bells
Up through the mystic forest climbing,
⠀⠀Down-floating o'er the fells,
Enwall me and hold me,
⠀⠀⠀⠀La Verna.⠀⠀⠀⠀⠀H. E. G. ROPE

106

62

St. Francis's Farewell to Mount La Verna

PAX XPI

" JESUS, MARY, my hope. I, Fra Masseo a sinner, and unworthy servant of Jesus Christ, Companion of Brother Francis of Assisi, a man most pleasing in the sight of God :

" Peace and health to all the sons and brethren of the great Patriarch, Francis, standard-bearer of Christ : When the great Patriarch resolved to take leave of this Holy Mountain on the 30th day of September 1224, being the feast of St. Jerome, and of Count Orlando, the Count of Chinsi having sent him an ass to ride upon, for he could not put his feet to the ground because they were pierced and wounded by nails, in the morning early having heard Mass, according to his custom in St. Maria degli Angioli, he called us all into the Oratory and commended us, under obedience, to abide in charity, to be instant in prayer, to have a diligent care of the place, and to sing the Divine Office there day and night. Moreover, he commended the whole of the Sacred Mountain to us, exhorting all the brethren, both present and to come, that they should never suffer this place to be profaned, but should ever keep it honoured and reverenced, giving his blessing to all who might dwell there, and to all who should reverence and respect it. On the other hand, he said : ' Let all those be confounded who shall not respect this place : let them expect the chastisement they deserve at the hand of God.' To me he said : ' Fra Masseo, I would have you know that my purpose is that this place should ever be inhabited by

God-fearing Religious, the flower of my Order : therefore let all Superiors endeavour to place here the best of the brethren.   Ah-ah-ah ! Fra Masseo, I can say no more.' Then he enjoined and laid upon us, Frate Angelo, Fra Silvestro, Frate Illuminato, and Fra Masseo, that we should have an especial care of the place where the great Marvel of the Stigmata had taken place.   And when he had said this, he cried : ' Addio, addio, addio, Fra Masseo.'   And turning to Frate Angelo he said : ' Addio, addio, addio, Angelo ' ; and the like he also said to Frate Silvestro and Frate Illuminato. ' Rest in peace, my dearest children. May God bless you, my dearest sons. Farewell, I am leaving you in the body, but I leave my heart behind with you. I am going away with Fra Pecorello de Dio ; I am going to Santa Maria degli Angeli, and here I shall return no more. I am going, farewell, farewell to all ! Farewell, O Mountain ! Farewell, Mount La Verna ! Farewell, O Mountain of Angels ! Farewell, my best beloved : O best beloved, farewell ! Brother Falcon, I thank thee for thy charity thou didst use me—Addio, addio, Sasso Spicco ; alas ! I may revisit thee no more. Farewell, O Rock ! Farewell, farewell, farewell, great Rock that didst receive me into thy bowels, confounding the wiles of the Evil One ; alas ! we may meet no more. Farewell, Santa Maria degli Angeli ! O Mother of the Eternal Word, I commend to thee these my sons.'   And whilst our Dear Father was speaking thus, our eyes were shedding fountains of tears, and he departed, weeping likewise, taking with him our hearts, leaving us orphans indeed for the loss of such a father !

" I, Fra Masseo, have writ all this.   And may God bless us."

MR. MONTGOMERY CARMICHAEL's Version

THE LITTLE BROWN COMPANY

NOTE.—This letter is read in the Refectory at La Verna every 30th September, the anniversary of the Saint's departure. Many of the Frati know the " Addio " by heart, and sometimes the Cicerone at La Verna will repeat it to sympathetic visitors on the very spot where it was uttered. It is an experience sufficiently trying to the emotions. One of the most important features of the letter is that it proves beyond a doubt the stupendous miracle that St. Francis was preserved from death when thrown over the sheer cliff by the Evil Spirit, by the wall turning to soft wax, and affording him a hold for hands and feet.—M.C.

63

With Love on Mount Alvernia

LOVE, I have knocked, and knocked, and waited
    years. . . .
But You have opened all to me at last.
Replenishing parched eyes with flooding tears,
Making my grief nobler than in the past,
Humbler and more enlightened. Now in truth,
I can discern the Grace that drove me on
In my undisciplined but ardent youth,
To seek on earth the Kingdom you had won.
By fountains, in the sunshine, 'mid the flowers,
Through brambles, over stony hill-side ways,
In merry-making, and in stricken hours
To which your absence gave the length of days,
Creation ever spoke to me of You.
I saw great beauty twisted, dwarfed by man ;
But everywhere, I saw Your hand renew
The glory of an everlasting Plan.

" Ask," You had said. I asked, and waited years. . . .
Now, in blest solitude, You answer me
With gifts of wounds and selfless, perfect tears.
Your very wounds for me ! . . . Your agony ! . . .
Your scorching tears ! . . . A thousand years are brief
When Love makes answer, burns the last alloy—
And secretly, outside the world's belief,
The boy's heart of an old man leaps for joy.

ARMEL O'CONNOR
The Poor Man of Assisi

64

Aurea Dicta

" NOLI me tangere " is the only favour which the Saint asks the World.

O sane madness, which can find, in the sharpest austerities and truths, a present heaven : O mad sanity, which, in all the pleasures of earth, can find no testimony that there is any heaven at all !

He who renounces goods, house, wife, etc. for God's sake shall receive a hundredfold in this life, with life everlasting. But he who, having obtained this hundredfold return of all his natural delights transfigured, renounces this also, and acknowledges no consolation but his share in the agony of the Cross, shall shine for ever in heaven as a sun among the stars.   Yet even he cannot escape his temporal reward, but hyssop itself, in touching his lips, becomes honey.

Thus irresistibly by Gods embraced
Is she who boasts her more than mortal chaste.

God is the only reality, and we are real only so far as we are in His order, and He is in us.

Let me love Thee so that the honour, riches and pleasures of the World may seem unworthy even of hatred —may be not even encumbrances.

If we may credit certain hints contained in the lives of the Saints, love raises the spirit above the sphere of reverence and worship into one of laughter and dalliance ; a sphere in which the soul says :

Shall I the gnat, which dances in thy ray,
Dare to be reverent.

The mirth of the World is really the grin of despair.

COVENTRY PATMORE
The Rod, The Root, and the Flower
III

65
Founding of the Franciscan Monastery, Donegal

I

WHY rides the Ladye Nuala [1] o'er Galway's pleasant
    plain
  With such a host of Galloglach and Kerne in her
    train,
And beauteous ladies shining in the costly silks of Spain ?

II

The fathers of St. Francis in Rossreil cloister sate,
  And they pondered on the sanctity and fervour of
    their state.
When they saw a gallant companie ride towards the con-
    vent gate.

III

The sun flashed from the bright cathbarrs and harness
    dight with gold,
  And spear points thick as hazel-stems within a
    mountain wold,
And a lovely lady led the van, like Judith fam'd of old.

IV

" Oh ! tell us, noble lady, what brings this hosting here ?
  Why gleam upon this holy spot the deadly sword and
    spear—
None but Francis' blessed children 'neath our peaceful
    roof appear."

[1] Nuala was the daughter of O'Connor Faly, one of the most
powerful of the Leinster princes.

112

THE LITTLE BROWN COMPANY

V

" O ! holy father, we have come the bearers of a pray'r,
    Over many a rugged mountain and valley rich and
        fair,
To thy brethren who in cloistered cell thy founder's
    habit wear.

VI

" I am Lady Nuala, the wife of Hugh O'Donnel Roe,
    Whose banner waves where silvery Esk and mur-
        muring Erne flow,
Where the Saints of God liv'd and prayed, and died in
    days of long ago.

VII

" And they planted there a garden of sweetest scent and
    hue,
    Till the tempest came, and from its wings a pois'ning
        shadow threw,
And the weeds are now grown strong and rank—the
    flowers are only few.

VIII

" So come, O Blessed Father, and cast wide the seed again,
    That St. Patrick brought into our shores across the
        white-browed main,
And our Saviour watered with His blood in agony and pain.

IX

" And the Vesper hymn will rise once more beside our
    winding Bay,
    As the red sun steals beneath the wave to golden
        lands away,
And the white stars, like the Virgin's eyes, smile on the
    headlands grey.

X

" Oh ! come and gather in the flock from clifted shore and
hill,
And teach Tirconnell's gallant sons their heavenly
master's will,
And his blessing, like a moonlit mist, will rest above us
still."

XI

Thus answered then the fathers this noble lady's prayer—
" It pains us that unto your land we cannot now
repair,
Some future time, with God's good grace, we'll turn our
footsteps there."

XII

Deep sorrow darkened on the brow of Galloglach and
Kerne,
And the maiden faces drooped as droops the rain-
washed island fern,
Till the Lady raised her hand and spoke in angry tones
and stern.

XIII

" Then beware th' angrying wrath of God for every soul
that's lost,
Let it be for once and ever at your peril and your
cost,"
" Amen " rose wild and solemn from the white lips of the
host.

XIV

And the friars through the open gate came one, and two,
and three,
Till they stood within the centre of the noble
companie—
" We of our number, lady, will gladly follow thee."

114

THE LITTLE BROWN COMPANY

XV

Oh ! sweetly, sweetly did she smile and cast to heaven her
eyes,
To thank the Lord for blessing her saintly enterprise,
And a shout of gladness echoed to the laughing summer
skies.

XVI

So the joyful cohort travelled on their spreading distant
way,
Over rugged hills and valleys fair, for many and many
a day,
Till the sea wind kissed their weary brows by Donegal's
sweet Bay.

XVII

And thus the Lady Nuala with her noble chieftains all,
Raised the Convent of St. Francis by the waves of
Donegal,
Christ save her chaste and loving soul from Purgatorial
thrall.

LEO
*The Rise and Fall of the Irish
Franciscan Monasteries*

66

The Lady St. Clare

IN the city of Assisi was a wonderful woman, Clare by name, a woman full of virtue and born of true gentlefolk.

And in this city was born Master Saint Francis.

And the Lady St. Clare reigned with him in this earthly life and went with him into the eternal life.

Her father was a soldier, and all her lineage, by her father as by her mother, was drawn from soldiers.

Her father's house was abundant in goods and riches after the manner of that country.

Her mother was named Hortolana, that is to say, Gardener.

For she was to plant the garden of Holy Church with a plant full of good fruit. . . .

And after a little while she went to the church of St. Angelo in Panso. And when she saw that there she could not have perfect peace, she went to the church of St. Damiano by the counsel of Master Saint Francis. And her mind was possessed with the thought that never for any other thing would she remove from this place. . . .

In this little house which seemed like a cloister the Lady Saint Clare enclosed herself.

And for her the tempest of the world ceased and she secluded her body as long as she lived.

She may be called a silver dove, for thus does the dove make her nest, and her walls, and thus did she build herself in with other such little ones, there where she brought forth to God a great company of virgins.

THE LITTLE BROWN COMPANY

And she established the monastery and there founded her Order of Poor Ladies in the way of penitence.

Her first aim was that those who came after her should know her path and her footsteps.

In this narrow cloister she lived in great austerity and great discipline for the space of forty years.

And she mortified here the beauty of her body. She was all full of virtues, and Holy Church was filled with the odour of her good life.

Well may we say she lived gloriously who sees how many souls she gained to Our Lord.

Mrs. C. Balfour's Version
Life and Legends of St. Clare

67

Of St. Francis and the Ass

OUR Father, ere he went
    Out with his brother **Death**,
Smiling and well content
As a bridegroom goeth,
Sweetly forgiveness prayed
From man or beast whom he
Had ever injurèd
Or burdened needlessly.

" Verily," then said he,
" I crave before I pass
Forgiveness full and free
Of my little brother, the ass.
Many a time and oft,
When winds and ways were hot,
He hath borne me cool and soft
And service grudged me not.

" And once did it betide
There was unseen of me,
A gall upon his side
That suffered grievously.
And once his manger was
Empty and bare and brown.
(Please God for sweet, dry grass
That Bethlehem folk shook down ! ")

" Consider, brethren," said he,
" Our little brother ; how mild,

THE LITTLE BROWN COMPANY

How patient, he will be,
Though men are fierce and wild.
His coat is grey and fine,
His eyes are kind with love ;
This little brother of mine
Is gentle as the dove.

" Consider how such an one
Beheld our Saviour born,
And carried Him, full-grown,
Through Eastern streets one morn,
For this the Cross is laid
Upon him for a sign.
Greatly is honoured
This little brother of mine."

And even while he spake,
Down in the stable stall
His little ass 'gan shake
And turned its face to the wall.
Down fell the heavy tear ;
Its gaze so mournful was,
Fra Leo, standing near,
Pitied the little ass.

That night our father died,
All night the kine did low ;
The ass went misty-eyed,
With patient tears and slow.
The very birds on wings
Made mournful cries in the air.
Amen ! all living things
Our father's brethren were.

KATHARINE TYNAN HINKSON

68

The Death of St. Francis

THERE is something profoundly pathetic, and full of great problems, in the fact that at last, as it would seem, his flame of life leapt up and his heart rejoiced when they saw afar off on the Assisian hills the solemn pillars of the Portiuncula. He who had become a vagabond for the sake of a vision, he who had denied himself all sense of place and possession, he whose whole gospel and glory it was to be homeless, received like a Parthian shot from nature, the sting of the sense of home. He also had his *maladie du clocher*, his sickness of the spire; though his spire was higher than ours. " Never," he cried, with the sudden energy of strong spirits in death, " Never give up this place. If you would go anywhere or make any pilgrimage return always to your home, for this is the holy house of God." . . .

After he had taken farewell of some of his nearest, and especially some of his oldest, friends he was lifted at his own request off his own rude bed and laid on the bare ground, as some say clad only in a hair shirt as he had first gone forth into the wintry woods from the presence of his father. It was the final assertion of his great fixed idea; of praise and thanks springing to their most towering heights out of wickedness and nothing. As he lay there we may be certain that his teared and blinded eyes saw nothing but their object and origin. We may be sure that the soul in its last inconceivable isolation, was face to face with nothing less than God Incarnate and Christ Crucified. But for the men standing around him there must have been other thoughts mingling with these, and many memories must have gathered like ghosts in the twilight, as that day wore on and that great darkness descended in which we all lost a friend. . . . Round about him stood the brethren in their brown habits, those that had loved him even if they afterwards disputed with each other. . . . A man might fancy that the birds must have known when it happened and made some motion in the evening sky. As they had once, according to the tale, scattered to the four winds of heaven in the pattern of a cross at his signal of dispersion ; they might now have written in such dotted lines, a more awful augury across the sky.

Hidden in the woods perhaps were little crawling creatures never again to be so much noticed and under-stood, and it has been said that animals are sometimes conscious of things to which man their spiritual superior is for the moment blind. We do not know whether any shiver passed through all the thieves and the outcasts and the outlaws, to tell them what had happened to him who never knew the nature of scorn. But at least in the passages and porches of the Portiuncula there was a sudden stillness when all the brown figures stood like little bronze statues, for the stopping of the great heart that had not broken till it held the world.

G. K. CHESTERTON
St. Francis of Assisi

69

After-Strain

(From *Ode to the Setting Sun*)

NOW with wan ray that other sun of song
    Sets in the blackening waters of my soul ;
One step, and lo ! the Cross stands gaunt and long
    'Twixt me and yet bright skies, a presaged dole.

Even so, O Cross ! thine is the Victory,
    Thy roots are fast within our fairest fields ;
Brightness may emanate in Heaven from thee,
    Here thy dread symbol only shadow yields.

Of reapèd joys thou art the heavy sheaf
    Which must be lifted though the reaper groan ;
Yea, we may cry till Heaven's ear be deaf,
    But we must bear thee, and must bear alone.

Vain were a Simon ; of the Antipodes
    Our night not borrows the superfluous day.
Yet woe to him that from his burden flees,
    Crushed in the face of what he cast away.

Therefore, O tender Lady, Queen Mary,
    Thou gentleness that dost enmoss and drape
The Cross's rigorous austerity,
    Wipe thou the blood from wounds that needs must
        gape.

Lo, though suns rise and set, but crosses stay,
    " I leave thee ever," saith she, " light of cheer."

THE LITTLE BROWN COMPANY

'Tis so : Yon sky still thinks upon the Day,
　　And showers aerial blossoms on his bier.

Yon cloud with wrinkled fire is edgèd sharp ;
　　And once more welling through the air, ah me !
How the sweet viol plains him to the harp,
　　Whose pangèd sobbings throng tumultuously.

Oh, this Medusa-pleasure with her stings !
　　This essence of all suffering, which is joy !
I am not thankless for the spell it brings,
　　Though tears must be told down for the charmèd toy.

No, while soul, sky, and music bleed together,
　　Let me give thanks even for those griefs in me,
The restless, windward stirrings of whose feather
　　Prove them the brood of immortality.

My soul is quitted of death-neighbouring swoon,
　　Who shall not stake her immitigable scars
Until she hears " My sister ! " from the moon,
　　And takes the kindred kisses of the stars.

FRANCIS THOMPSON

70

St. Francis and the World

ST. FRANCIS was a poet and a dreamer with all the exquisite tenderness and sensibility of those in whom life expresses itself by feeling and emotion. But unlike the poet, pure and simple, the Saint possessed the dynamic spiritual power to translate his frail dreams into mighty realities. In the process of emptying his heart of everything that might stand between himself and God he, in very truth, became invested with the power and capacity for loving all God's creation. He who would deny himself the love of creatures that he might become God's great lover, by Divine equity becomes the lover, and beloved, of all. Everything, everywhere, God and His transcendent Presence and reflection giving, and clamouring for, love. He who would give up all, a thousand unlooked for joys are thrust upon him. Even the world that the Saint flees from, refusing its mean bribes, becomes his subject and suppliant. The world professing to despise the qualities which go to make the Saint, in spite of itself, or, perhaps, because it is what it is, ends by reverencing.

The great figures who pass through the shadowy aisles of history, kings, warriors, statesmen, are forgotten. They lived and worked for mortal things, and mortality is inexorable. It pays in time-currency. But the Saints whom the World, in its blindness of perversity, could neither understand nor reward, humanity is compelled to enshrine.

The history makers who used the solid material of earth are phantoms. St. Francis and his kindred, who lived

124

and had their being in the unseen, whose thoughts and actions were wrought of incorporeal substance, dominate and inspire the generations. They become arch-types of the highest and best that men can achieve, and fallen humanity takes heart of grace in seeing to what heights it can rise when God upholds and leads.

LOUIS VINCENT

71

Of Impatience which brings all our Gains to Nothing

I LABOURED long, I strove with might and main :
  And yet I cannot keep the good I gain.

Yea, I have been a monk full many a year,
Have suffered much, and wandered far and near,
Have sought and found—yet held not,—till I fear
That nothing can I show for all my pain.

In calm retreats my truest joy I found :
I strove in prayer, with no uncertain sound ;
I fed the poor for many miles around :
In sickness very patient have I lain.

In uttermost obedience did I dwell,
In suffering and poverty as well ;
Yea, I was chaste and happy in my cell,
So far my poor powers could attain.

To pray, I daily rose before the sun ;
Mass did I hear before the dark was done ;
To tierce and nones and vespers would I run,
And, after compline, still to watch was fain.

And then was said to me a scornful word !
—Deep in my heart that poisoned arrow stirred,—
At once my tongue was ready, when I heard,
With fierce and burning fury to complain.

126

THE LITTLE BROWN COMPANY

Now see how great and healthy I must be !
I heap my gains for all the world to see ;
Yet one poor word so fiercely angers me,
That I must strive to pardon it in vain !

FRA JACOPONE DA TODI
(From the translation
by MRS. THEODORE BECK)

72

Farewell to Assisi

IN the evening, not long after the Angelus rang, just as I was thinking I should go to rest early, the bells of Assisi struck up, calling to me in their festive notes, jubilant and yet solemn. San Francesco's bells went on ringing and ringing. Up there on the hill stood San Francesco's Convent, with all its windows lighted up ; and almost before I knew what I was doing I was on my way to the convent, whose bells were ringing and whose lights were gleaming. I felt I must go up once more to Assisi ; I must once more experience the singular, intoxicating charm of the streets, those steep alleys, those unpaved ways and open squares.

So on and on I went until I got up there and could wander about everywhere unnoticed and unknown, visiting all the spots that were so dear to me : the square in front of Santa Chiara ; the road with the wide vista of the open country beyond the Porta Nuova ; the steep narrow alley leading up to Santa Audrea ; all the localities rich in memories and associations—all of which I was to leave behind me on the morrow and which I should perhaps never revisit. Once more I passed by the green gate of St. Philomena's little convent, and lingered before the grating, thinking of the brothers who were calmly reciting their Latin night prayers within, as they would do on the morrow when I should be no longer there, as they would be doing should I return thither some time or other after the lapse of years.

At length I tore myself away. At the corner where the high-road to Assisi turns off to the church and monastery, I sent back a last, longing look. High up above I saw under an arch in the wall the swinging lantern whose light had often shone upon me of an evening in days long past, when I sat at my window listening to the conflicting voices within me. Only one woman dressed in black came noiselessly down the narrow, deserted street, and I heard the purling of the brook. Farewell, Assisi—Assisi mio, farewell.

JOHANNES JÖRGENSEN
Pilgrim Walks in Franciscan Italy

73
A Prayer to the Humble on Earth and to the Triumphant in Heaven

PRAY for me, pray for me,
  Ye who tread the stony way,
Clad in your humility,
Pilgrim's vesture, sad and grey.
Pray that I your path may keep,
And with you, rejoice and weep.

Pray for me, pray for me,
Ye, for whom the pilgrim's dress
Is changed to robes of dignity
Befitting halls of holiness :
Pray that I may yet find place
Where the humble see His face.

FATHER ADRIAN, O.F.M.

74

From the Prayers said in Franciscan Churches on the Feast of St. Francis

LET us recount with praise those signs of holiness so sweet and wondrous displayed by blessed Francis ; he who to those that enrolled themselves in his flock gave a new Rule, re-enjoining Christ the King's commandments.

. . . .

Their habit is coarse, their girdle harsh, feet are unshod, food is scanty, purse and goods are cast aside ; for Francis disdains earthly riches, poverty is all he craves for.

. . . .

He seeks a place of tears, where, in bitterness of heart, he weeps over all the precious time lost in the world. In the loneliness of a mountain cave he weeps prostrate on the earth ; till at length he is comforted.

. . . .

Then to him from on high there descends the Royal Seraph ; and while Francis gazes in sad and trembling amazement, on his flesh are imprinted the blistering marks of Christ's Passion.

. . . .

O thrice-happy Francis, Father most loving, let those marks of the Cross which Thou hast borne, let Christ through whom thou hast triumphantly overcome the world, the flesh, and the devil, shelter us from danger and protect us in adversity ; that we too may, in company with our brethren, some day enjoy the promised Reward in the glory of our heavenly home.

. . . . . .

O may all thy Franciscan Children attain to the everlasting joys. Amen. Alleluia.

THE MISSAL

O FRANCIS, never may thy sainted name
     Be thought or written save with soul aflame,
Nor spoken openly, nor breathed apart
Without a stir or swelling of the heart :
O mate of Poverty ! O pearl unpriced,
O co-espoused, co-transforate with Christ.

                              W. H. MEYERS

ACKNOWLEDGEMENTS

MY thanks are due and are here gratefully ten-
dered to Father Cuthbert, O.S.F.C., Father
H. E. G. Rope, M.A., Mr. Montgomery Carmichael
and Mr. Wilkinson Sherren, each of whom has been
specially kind and helpful. Also to the following writers
and publishers who have permitted me to include their
work :

Messrs. Burns, Oates & Washbourne, Ltd., for poems
by Alice Meynell, Katharine Tynan, Aubrey De Vere,
Francis Thompson, and prose extracts by Montgomery
Carmichael and Miss Lockhart. To Mrs. Hinkson I
am particularly indebted for unusual kindness in giving
me free choice ; Messrs. Sands & Co. for confirming
the permission so graciously given by Miss Enid Dinnis,
Father Cuthbert, O.S.F.C., and for the right to use a poem
by Miss Rosa Mulholland and excerpts from Johannes
Jörgensen and Father Dominic Devas, O.F.M. ; Messrs.
Longmans, Green & Co. for the quotations from
Father Cuthbert, O.S.F.C., Mrs. C. Balfour and Mr.
T. O'Connor Sloane's translation of Jörgensen's *Life
of St. Francis*. Mr. G. K. Chesterton, his agents
A. P. Watt & Son, Ltd., and his publishers Messrs.
Hodder & Stoughton, for two selections from Mr.
Chesterton's *St Francis*. I am further indebted to Messrs.
Hodder & Stoughton for the Paul Sabatier extract.
Messrs. Dent, the famous " Everyman " publishers, for
several courtesies.

Mrs. Theodore Beck for allowing me a free hand with
her beautiful translations of the poems of Fra Jacopone

134

ACKNOWLEDGEMENTS

da Todi ; Father H. E. G. Rope and his publishers Messrs. Heath Cranton for several poems by the priestly laureate ; Mrs. H. G. Patmore and Messrs. Geo. Bell, for the Coventry Patmore page ; The MacMillan Company of America for a fragment by Vachell Lindsay and the poem by Charles L. O'Donnell ; Messrs. George Allen & Unwin, Ltd., and the Ruskin Trustees for the Ruskin quotations. The Dolphin Press of Philadelphia, publishers of the American Ecclesiastical Review, for kindly seconding the permission freely accorded me by Father Paschal Robinson, O.F.M., the distinguished Franciscan scholar ; The Bodley Head for confirming Mrs. Helen Parry Eden's consent ; the Oxford University Press and Mr. Gerard Hopkins for a characteristic example of Father Hopkins' genius ; Mr. Armel O'Connor, the authentic voice of Franciscan poesy ; the unknown R. E.

Sister Mary Benvenuta, O.P., and the Mother Prioress at All Souls' Priory, Headington, for assent granted with fine Dominican courtesy. Messrs. Basil Blackwell of Oxford for acquiescing to the requests of Miss Enid Dinnis and Miss Madeleine Nightingale, and to both these talented ladies for making the way easier. Mr. J. B. Morton for a delightful poem rescued from the files of the *Sunday Express* ; The Franciscan Fathers for the liberal use I have made of the Fioretta. Father Conrad Walmsley, O.F.M., for bringing the work of the late Father Adrian, O.F.M., to my notice and many other helpful favours ; Father Stanislaus, O.S.F.C., for his helpful co-operation ; Mr. W. E. Awde and the Catholic Social Guild.

The Rev. H. F. B. MacKay and the Society of SS. Peter and Paul for the quotations from Mr. MacKay's beautiful study of St. Francis ; Miss Nancy Dustan, Mr. Alan G. M'Dougall.

Mr. Edward Hutton and Messrs. Methuen for the extract from *The Cities of Umbria*, and also to the editors

ACKNOWLEDGEMENTS

of *The Franciscan Monthly, Franciscan Annals, La Vie Seraphique, Catholic World, Ave Maria, The Christian Democrat, The Month,* in whose pages several of the poems included first appeared.

If, through inadvertence, I have omitted any acknowledgements, I humbly beg the indulgence of the authors.

L. V.

PRINTED IN GREAT BRITAIN BY ROBERT MACLEHOSE AND CO. LTD.
THE UNIVERSITY PRESS, GLASGOW.

19